PRAYERS that RELEASE HEAVEN & MOVE MOUNTAINS

JOHN ECKHARDT

CHARISMA
HOUSE

Most CHARISMA HOUSE BOOK GROUP products are available at special quantity discounts for bulk purchase for sales promotions, premiums, fund-raising, and educational needs. For details, write Charisma House Book Group, 600 Rinehart Road, Lake Mary, Florida 32746, or telephone (407) 333-0600.

PRAYERS THAT RELEASE HEAVEN AND MOVE MOUNTAINS by John Eckhardt
Published by Charisma House
Charisma Media/Charisma House Book Group
600 Rinehart Road
Lake Mary, Florida 32746
www.charismahouse.com

Book 2

Prayers that Move Mountains

John Eckhardt

CHARISMA
HOUSE

CONTENTS

Contents

INTRODUCTION

BE THOU REMOVED!

For assuredly, I say to you, whoever says to this mountain, "Be removed and be cast into the sea," and does not doubt in his heart, but believes that those things he says will come to pass, he will have whatever he says. Therefore I say to you, whatever things you ask when you pray, believe that you receive them, and you will have them.

—MARK 11:23–24

WHAT MOUNTAIN ARE you facing in this season of life? Unemployment? Financial problems? Difficult marriage? Illness? Foreclosure? Undefeated sin? Whatever it is, the power lies in you to speak to that mountain and say, "Be thou removed!"

The keys to deliverance, freedom, and the abundant life have been given back to us. Jesus came to return to us our authority in the earth so that we can exercise prayer and faith to bring God's will from the heavenly realm into the earth realm, affecting our lives in the here and now.

The Bible says that you can decree and declare things with your mouth, and they will happen (Rom. 4:17). According to Joshua 1:8, you have the power to make your way prosperous, to mow down the mountains in your way. By mediating and obeying the Word of God, you put yourself in a place of life and blessing. Choice is where your power lies. What you choose to speak and declare needs to coincide with how you live and what you meditate on.

The characteristic of a righteous person is faith in God. You have to know God in order to have faith in Him. The key to moving mountains is really knowing God and dwelling in His presence. The just live by faith in God and do not trust in their own abilities or what someone else can do on their behalf. Jesus said it: "Have faith in God" (Mark 11:22).

Don't lift your problems to such a level that they become your idol. You serve a big God who is faithful to deliver His people out of all their troubles (Ps. 34:17, 19). Walk in faith. Prayer can change things. Worship can change things. Your faith can move mountains. You'll prosper even in bad times. Your prosperity is not dependent on the Dow Jones Industrial Average, NASDAQ, or mortgage rates. Your prosperity is dependent on God. Be a giver. Be a worshiper. Be obedient. Live clean. God will prosper you. God will bless you.

When He put all those plagues on the Egyptians in the land of Goshen, nothing fell on the Jews. They were protected from all the locust, plagues, and judgment. Ask God to put a Goshen anointing on you. It may be falling on this one and that one. It may be dark over there, but you are going to have sun. Locusts may be eating up everyone else's stuff, but you are going to have rain fall on your crops, because you are under the protection of God. "He who dwells in the secret place of the Most High shall abide under the shadow of the Almighty.... A thousand may fall at your side, and ten thousand at your right hand; but it shall not come near you" (Ps. 91:1, 7), because you walk by faith. You don't walk by what you see.

Put your trust in God. Have faith in God where you can say to your mountain, "Be thou removed and cast into the sea," and if you do not doubt in your heart, but believe that whatever you say will come to pass, you will have whatever you say.

In this book I am going to teach you how to speak to mountains and whatever stands in your way. You will learn how to say, "Be removed!" Your faith in a big God is the key to this. If you speak in faith, your faith can move mountains. When stuff gets in your way, speak to it. There is no government program that can move your mountain and no such thing as removemymountain .com. No! You speak. You learn how to walk and live by faith. Don't get depressed and caught up into financial mountains and other problems that can weigh you down. You have the power to move mountains.

God always sits on the throne. Salvation is not only about going to heaven, but it's also about ruling and reigning in your authority on earth. It's about living in the kingdom of God. We are living in the age of the kingdom now—the age of salvation, deliverance, grace, glory, power, and prosperity. Your faith is the key to bringing it all to pass.

Faith Declarations

Because of Christ I am free, and whom the Son sets free is free indeed.

I do not put my trust in man. I do not put my trust in flesh. I put my trust in God.

I live by faith. I walk by faith and not by sight.

I am responsible for my decisions and my choices. I make a decision. I choose life. I choose blessings. I choose the Word of God. I choose wisdom.

I thank You, Lord, that I am responsible for making my own way prosperous and having good success.

I have faith to speak to mountains, and they will obey me.

My heart will never depart from You, Lord. I will always serve God.

Thank You, Lord, for prosperity. I will flourish because I live in the days of the Messiah.

I will have prosperity and good success because of God's grace, in Jesus's name.

Prayers That Demolish Mountains*

I speak to every mountain in my life and command it to be removed and cast into the sea (Mark 11:23).

I speak to every financial mountain to be removed from my life in the name of Jesus.

Let every evil mountain hear the voice of the Lord and be removed (Mic. 6:2).

I prophesy to the mountains and command them to hear the Word of the Lord and be removed (Ezek. 36:4).

Let the mountains tremble at the presence of God (Hab. 3:10).

I contend with every mountain and command them to hear my voice (Mic. 6:1).

Lay the mountain of Esau (the flesh) to waste (Mal. 1:3).

Put forth Your hand, O Lord, and overturn the mountains by the roots (Job 28:9).

I speak to every mountain of debt to be removed and cast into the sea. Lord, You are against every destroying mountain (Jer. 51:25).

---

* From John Eckhardt, *Prayers That Rout Demons* (Lake Mary, FL: Charisma House, 2008), 43.

Let the mountains melt at Your presence, O God (Judg. 5:5, KJV).

_____

Make waste the evil mountains in my life, O Lord (Isa. 42:15).

_____

I thresh every mountain, I beat them small, and I make the hills as chaff (Isa. 41:15).

_____

Every mountain in my way will become a plain (Zech. 4:7).

_____

CHAPTER 1

THE PRAYER OF FAITH

And the prayer of faith will save the sick,
and the Lord will raise him up. And if he
has committed sins, he will be forgiven.

—JAMES 5:15

And whatever things you ask in prayer,
believing, you will receive.

—MATTHEW 21:22

Without faith it is impossible to please Him,
for he who comes to God must believe that
He is, and that He is a rewarder of those
who diligently seek Him.

—HEBREWS 11:6

THE PRAYER OF faith is bold and prayed from a sure
foundation of faith. The person praying this prayer is
assured of God's will for the situation or issue at hand.
They are confident and hopeful, knowing that it is God's

will to answer their prayer. "The prayer of faith has power. The prayer of faith has trust. The prayer of faith has healing for body and soul."[1]

The New Testament church was in the midst of this kind of prayer when they were praying for Peter. Right in the middle of their prayer they heard a knock on the door, and there was Peter. They were in awe. Many other examples of this prayer can be seen throughout the ministries of Jesus, the apostles, and in our lives today. The apostles prayed knowing what the will of God was for the situations they faced.

Many believers fear that when we leave things to the "will of God," somehow the solution, provision, healing, or deliverance they need will not be given. But they don't know the will of God for them. According to the model prayer that Jesus gave His disciples in Matthew 6:9–11, we are to pray for God's will to be done. But people "resign their intelligence at that point to the unknown God....It does not say, 'If it be thy will' and stop there. There is a comma there, not a period. The prayer is this, 'Thy will be done, as in heaven, so in earth' (Luke 11:2)."[2] I'd say that is a significant difference.

FAITH IN GOD'S WILL

When we pray the prayer of faith, we are praying God's will for how things are in heaven to be done in the earth realm. Here is where a clear revelation of the kingdom is very important. Is there sickness in heaven? Is there lack in heaven? Are there any unsaved in heaven? We must have faith to believe that God wants His will for our health, prosperity, and full salvation to be manifested not only when we go to heaven but even as we dwell on earth. It's for His glory. When people see that God's people have His ear and He is answering their prayers, that is a testimony for Him. People are drawn to God when they can see through His witnesses that He is a God who hears, and if He hears, they know He will answer.

Jesus said, "I have come that they may have life, and that they may have it more abundantly" (John 10:10). You have to gain the assurance that is God's will for you, so when you pray, you will pray with confidence and faith that He will answer you.

> The Lord wants us to have more faith. When several are praying together for the same petition and one has prayed the prayer of faith, the Holy Ghost will glorify Jesus by witnessing the prayer that is heard.... The Lord wants us to know that He has heard us. We need to thank and praise Him for answering and that will help us a great deal when we pray.[3]
>
> —WILLIAM SEYMOUR

WONDER-WORKING FAITH

There are many different kinds of faith: (1) faith that gets you saved, (2) general faith in whatever appears real to you, (3) faith that God is real, (4) faith that your chair won't break when you sit in it, and so on. But what I am talking about in this chapter is another kind of faith—a special faith. The Amplified Bible reads, "To another [wonder-working] faith by the same [Holy] Spirit" (1 Cor. 12:9). This faith, also called special faith, is one of the spiritual gifts. Smith Wigglesworth said that you often find that if you will make a step of faith and use your own faith that you as an individual Christian have, when you come to the end of that faith, very often this supernatural faith will take over. The reason it hasn't happened with a lot of folks is that they don't first use what they already have.

> Every believer already has general faith or saving faith, which is also a gift. Ephesians 2:8 says, "For by grace are ye saved through faith; and that not of yourselves: it is the gift of God."
>
> The faith that you are saved by is a gift of God, but it is not one of the nine gifts of the Spirit. Saving faith is given to you through hearing the Word, because the Bible says, "So then faith [saving faith] cometh by hearing, and hearing by the word of God" (Rom. 10:17).
>
> The faith we are talking about—"special faith"—is something other than general faith or saving faith. It is a supernatural manifestation of the Holy Spirit whereby a believer is empowered with special faith, or wonder-working faith, and it is beyond simple saving faith.[4]

This is the kind of faith that you need to be able to move the obstructions and obstacles in your way. Sickness, financial strife, abuse, pride, unemployment, bondages, and strongholds of all kinds will not be able to stay in your life when you pray with wonder-working faith. They must go!

All you have to do is believe, and nothing will be impossible for you (Mark 9:23). That is special. Special faith will cause you to speak to stubborn demons and say, "I command you, come out of him and enter him no more!" (v. 25). Special faith is the miracle-working faith that Jesus had during His ministry on the earth, and He said that we would walk in even greater power and perform greater things than He did.

PROPHESY TO YOUR MOUNTAIN

I am reminded of the passage in Ezekiel where God instructed the prophet to prophesy to a valley of dry bones. While Ezekiel had no comparison in the natural that what God was asking him to do was possible, he had an unshakable faith in the God who commanded him.

> And He said to me, "Son of man, can these bones live?" So I answered, "O Lord GOD, You know." Again He said to me, "Prophesy to these bones, and say to them, '*O dry bones, hear the word of the Lord!*'...So I prophesied as I was commanded; and as I prophesied, there was a noise, and suddenly a rattling; and the bones came together, bone to bone. Indeed, as I looked, the sinews and the flesh came upon them, and the skin covered them over...and breath came

into them, and they lived, and stood upon their feet, an exceedingly great army.

—EZEKIEL 37:3–10, EMPHASIS ADDED

Can your mountain hear you prophesying to it the Word of the Lord? I challenge you to begin to incorporate the prayer of faith and begin to prophesy to your mountain. Say to it, "Mountain, the Word says that if I believe, nothing will be impossible to me. Mountain, I believe the Word of the Lord. And the Word of the Lord to you today is BE THOU REMOVED and cast into the sea!"

Even if you have never seen deliverance, healing, or breakthrough in your life or family before, know that today is a new day and that your faith in the power of God will make the impossible possible for you.

PRAYERS THAT RELEASE SPECIAL FAITH*

I declare that I, like Enoch, have a testimony that I please God through my faith (Heb. 11:5).

Because of my faith I am pleasing to God, and He will reward me because I seek after Him diligently (Heb. 11:6).

By faith I will sojourn in the land of promise, as in a strange country, dwelling in tabernacles with Isaac and Jacob, as I am an heir of the same promise (Heb. 11:9).

---

* Some prayers are from John Eckhardt, *Prayers That Bring Healing* (Lake Mary, FL: Charisma House, 2010), 61–63.

I will forsake any bondage that seeks to entrap me, looking forward by faith and setting my eyes on Him who is invisible (Heb. 11:27).

I decree and declare that by faith I will walk through my trials on dry ground, and my enemies will be drowned (Heb. 11:29).

I will encircle the immovable walls in my life, and by my faith those walls will fall down (Heb. 11:30).

Like Rahab, I will receive the men of God with peace. I will not perish with those who do not believe (Heb. 11:31).

I will subdue kingdoms, rain down righteousness, obtain promises, and stop the mouths of lions because of my faith (Heb. 11:33).

I declare that I will not only receive a good testimony of faithfulness, but I will also receive all that God has promised (Heb. 11:39–40).

I am established and anointed by God (2 Cor. 1:21).

I activate my mustard seed of faith and say to this mountain of sickness and disease in my life, "Be removed and go to another place." Nothing will be impossible to me (Matt. 17:20).

Because You have anointed me, I have faith and do not doubt that I can speak to any illness, curse it at the root, and cause it to dry up and die, just as You did to the fig tree. I also know that if I tell to this mountain of sickness that is in my way to move and be cast into the sea, it shall be done (Matt. 21:21).

I declare that I have uncommon, great faith in the power of Jesus Christ, faith that cannot be found anywhere else (Matt. 8:10).

Just as Jesus stood in the boat and spoke to the storm, I too can stand in the midst of the storms in my life and rebuke the winds and the waves to command calmness in my life. My faith overrides all my fears (Matt. 8:26).

I will not sink into faithlessness and doubt; I will be upheld by the mighty hand of God (Matt. 14:31).

I pray as Your anointed disciples prayed, "Increase my faith!" (Luke 17:5).

I will not be weak in faith. Like Abraham, I declare that my body is not dead but alive to birth out the gifts and anointing God has set aside for me (Rom. 4:19).

I will not stagger at the promise of God through unbelief, but I will stand strong in the faith, giving glory to God (Rom. 4:20).

My faith increases the more I hear, and hear by the Word of God (Rom. 10:17).

Even though I go through many common trials in this life, God, I declare that You are faithful. You will not allow me to face things beyond what I can stand. You have ordered a way of escape for me, and through Your strength I can bear it (1 Cor. 10:13).

I walk by faith and not by sight (2 Cor. 5:7).

I declare that I feel the substance and see the evidence of the things that I have faith for (Heb. 11:1).

You are Lord of all, and the worlds were framed by Your very words. You spoke into existence unseen things (Heb. 11:3).

I see through the eyes of faith the promise of things afar off. I am persuaded of their reality. I embrace them, knowing that I am a stranger and pilgrim on this earth (Heb. 11:13).

I will stand firm and not waver. I will come boldly before God, asking in faith (James 1:6).

I will not suffer shipwreck in my life, because I have faith and a good conscience (1 Tim. 1:19).

I thank You, God, that the testing of my faith produces patience to wait for Your Word to manifest in my life (James 1:3).

I hold the mystery of faith with a pure conscience (1 Tim. 3:9).

I declare that my faith works together with my works, and by my works my faith is made perfect (James 2:22).

I will show my faith by the works I do (James 2:18).

I am blessed with believing Abraham because I am a person of faith (Gal. 3:9).

By faith the walls built up around the territory God has promised to me will fall like the walls of Jericho (Heb. 11:30).

Because of my faith in Jesus I have boldness and confident access to approach God (Eph. 3:12).

I am a son of Abraham because I have faith (Gal. 3:7).

I am a son of God because I have faith in Christ Jesus (Gal. 3:26).

I go in peace because my faith has saved me (Luke 7:50).

My faith is alive (James 2:17).

The Spirit of God has given me the gift of faith (1 Cor. 12:9).

I have faith in God (Mark 11:22).

Let it be to me according to my faith (Matt. 9:29).

No man has dominion over my faith. I stand by faith (2 Cor. 1:24).

Like Stephen, I do great wonders and signs because I am full of faith (Acts 6:8).

I will arise and go my way, because my faith has made me well (Luke 17:19).

I receive my sight; my faith has made me well (Luke 18:42).

My faith is not in the wisdom of men but in the power of God (1 Cor. 2:5).

I will not be sluggish. I will imitate those who through faith and patience inherit the promises of God (Heb. 6:12).

The just shall live by faith (Rom. 1:17).

The righteousness of God is revealed to me through faith in Jesus (Rom. 3:22).

I am justified by my faith in Jesus (Rom. 3:26).

I have access by faith to the grace of God (Rom. 5:2).

I am raised to life through faith in Christ (Col. 2:12).

I do not fear the wrath of the king, and by faith I forsake Egypt (Heb. 11:27).

By faith I receive the promise of God in my life (Gal. 3:22).

My faith and hope are in God (1 Pet. 1:21).

My faith will not fail (Luke 22:32).

By faith the promise of God is sure to me, the seed of Abraham (Rom. 4:16).

I pray the prayer of faith and will see the sick saved and raised up (James 5:15).

I take the shield of faith and quench all the fiery darts of the wicked one (Eph. 6:16).

I put on the breastplate of faith and love (1 Thess. 5:8).

I obtain for myself good standing and great boldness in my faith in Christ Jesus (1 Tim. 3:13).

The Holy Scriptures make me wise for salvation through faith in Christ Jesus (2 Tim. 3:15).

The sharing of my faith is effective because I acknowledge that every good thing that is in me is because of Jesus (Philem. 1:6).

I am justified by my faith in Christ (Gal. 2:16).

I am rich in faith and an heir to the kingdom (James 2:5).

I contend earnestly for the faith that was delivered to me (Jude 3).

The Word profits me well because I mix what I have heard with faith (Heb. 4:2).

Like Abel, I offer an excellent sacrifice to God because of my faith (Heb. 11:4).

I please God, and He rewards me because I have faith (Heb. 11:6).

By faith I obey and go out to the place I will receive as an inheritance (Heb. 11:8).

By faith I dwell in the land of promise (Heb. 11:9).

CHAPTER 2

THE PRAYER OF THE RIGHTEOUS

The effective, fervent prayer of a righteous man avails [accomplishes] much.

—JAMES 5:16

THE CONDITION OF the heart is a major aspect of answered prayer. It is sincere prayer from the heart that makes the power of God available. The Amplified Version of James 5:16 reads, "The earnest (heartfelt, continued) prayer of a righteous man makes tremendous power available [dynamic in its working]." James is encouraging the believers by the example of Elijah, who was a man subject to the same passions as any man, yet his prayer shut up the heavens: "Elijah was a man with a nature like ours, and he prayed earnestly that it would not rain; and it did not rain on the land for three years and six months. And he prayed again, and the heaven gave rain, and the earth produced its fruit" (vv. 17–18).

Elijah was known for his fervency. *Fervent* means having or showing great emotion or zeal, ardent, extremely hot or glowing. Many try to divorce emotion from prayer, but God responds to those who are sincere and ardent. The implication is that those who are righteous will pray this way. This is because righteousness stirs us to pray for justice, equity, fairness, and the things that are right.

Righteous people will have a passion in prayer. When they open their mouths and begin to pray and speak to the mountains in their lives, wisdom, life, truth, and justice flow out. Their environment begins to take on the attributes of the kingdom as they speak it into existence.

Righteousness is the foundation for the kingdom of God. In order for the kingdom of God—righteousness, peace, and joy in the Holy Spirit (Rom. 14:17)—to be manifested in your life, you must be righteous. His kingdom comes and His will is done when a righteous person prays.

The Lord's eyes and ears are on the righteous. He hears their prayers and answers them. He rewards the righteous and saves them out of all their troubles. God seeks to level the mountains of the righteous. He seeks to make roads in the wilderness and rivers in the desert for the righteous. He will do this for you just as He did for Daniel:

> In those days I, Daniel, was mourning three full weeks. I ate no pleasant food, no meat or wine came into my mouth, nor did I anoint myself at all, till three whole weeks were fulfilled.... Suddenly, a hand touched me...and he said to me, "O Daniel,

man greatly beloved, understand the words that I speak to you, and stand upright, for I have now been sent to you....Do not fear, Daniel, for from the first day that you set your heart to understand, and to humble yourself before your God, your words were heard; and I have come because of your words."

—Daniel 10:2, 10–12

The Lord will send angelic reinforcement to help you stand and be victorious over the evil forces that seek to destroy God's Word over your life. Daniel prayed with fervency and passion, and his prayer was effective—it accomplished much! An angel of the Lord came to him, strengthened him, and delivered a prophetic word so powerful that it is still being activated and fulfilled for the body of Christ today.

WHO ARE THE RIGHTEOUS?

The righteous are those who are in right standing with God. Because of Christ we can all stand upright in the presence of God and boldly make our requests known to Him—if we have accepted His sacrifice. The righteous are bold as a lion.

The righteous are those who have and occupy—or take up residence in—the kingdom of heaven. The Bible says that the righteous shine in the kingdom of their Father. Light and gladness shine on their path. They may have many afflictions, but God delivers them out of them all.

The righteous have the mind of Christ. Their thoughts are right and pure. They keep a sober mind. They do not claim or trust in their own righteousness, but they live under the imputed righteousness of Christ. They are open to the correction of the Lord and His ministers. They receive wise counsel and apply it to their lives.

The righteous are immovable and unable to be uprooted out of their place in God. Their house will stand. Their children will be saved, blessed, and have plenty to eat. They will flourish and will not be overthrown by the enemy. They will not be led astray by discouragement, doubt, or depression. The righteous are sure that God will come and save them.

The righteous are generous and merciful. They are concerned and care for the poor. They are active in areas of justice. They seek justice. They walk with integrity. Enduring riches and honor are with them. They are fruitful, and their labors lead to life.

The righteous welcome godly associations and wisdom. They know who is around them. They are careful with whom they let into their inner circle. People who associate with wickedness and ungodliness can hinder you from breaking through. Your association with them can lead you to a place of ineffectiveness in the spirit. Your words and prayers will not move mountains because your association with them has led you astray (Prov. 12:26). Sometimes you have to tell your friends and crooked business partners to go.

When you find yourself coming up against a block in the spirit, take a look around at your friends. The Bible says, "Do not be unequally yoked with unbelievers." They may even be the open door to some of the stubborn demons and strongholds you are struggling with. Be wise. Let the counsel of the ungodly be far from you (Job 22:18, AMP).

THE RIGHTEOUS AND THE COVENANT OF GOD

You are "the righteous" and can claim all the benefits of the righteous by being in covenant with God. God doesn't haphazardly bless people. He doesn't just bless people for any reason. God blesses those with whom He is in covenant. Being in covenant with God is a contract or a promise of His peace, safety, favor, protection, health, and prosperity. And God does not break His promises or go back on His Word (Num. 23:19; Isa. 55:11).

Covenant with God is a mutual blessing. God gets a people, and we get God (Lev. 26:12). We become the righteousness of God through Christ Jesus (Rom. 3:22). Because we have received the new covenant through His shed blood on the cross, His righteousness is imputed to, or counted toward, us. We become "the righteous." But if we don't remain in God and give ourselves over to Him completely, He doesn't have "a people." Then there is no need for the covenant. We cannot be God's own if we do not walk according to His covenant. He cannot claim us and put His name on us. We can pray for peace in the storm and speak to mountains all year long, but without Jesus, who is the Prince of Peace and the waymaker, peace will not come and mountains will not be removed.

The righteous possess the kingdom of God (Matt. 5:10). Are you righteous? This goes beyond being saved. Righteousness is about continually living right before God. This is not about perfection. It's about your lifestyle being that of a righteous person. A righteous person does not live a sinful lifestyle. The righteous walk at a level of holiness and integrity. They are not liars, drunkards, and whoremongers. They don't mistreat people. If you are righteous, then the words you speak over your situation will have effect. They will cause things to line up for you in the Spirit. Your covenant with God is everlasting, and you will not fall, for He has imputed His righteousness to you through His Son, Jesus.

DECLARATIONS OF THE RIGHTEOUS

I will enter through the gate of the Lord (Ps. 118:20).

I am delivered from trouble (Prov. 11:8).

My root cannot be moved (Prov. 12:3).

I choose my friends carefully and will not be led astray (Prov. 12:26).

The memory of my name will be blessed, because I am righteous (Prov. 10:7).

My labor leads to life (Prov. 10:16).

I only desire good (Prov. 11:23).

My thoughts are right (Prov. 12:5).

My house will stand, and I will not be overthrown (Prov. 12:7).

I have a refuge in death and will not be banished (Prov. 14:32).

I walk in integrity, and my children are blessed (Prov. 20:7).

I do not covet greedily. I give and spare not (Prov. 21:26).

I am bold as a lion (Prov. 28:1).

I am not snared by transgression. I sing and rejoice (Prov. 29:6).

I consider the cause of the poor (Prov. 29:7).

I cry out, and the Lord hears. He delivers me out of all my troubles (Ps. 34:17).

I show mercy and give (Ps. 37:21).

I inherit the land and dwell in it forever (Ps. 37:29).

I speak wisdom, and my tongue talks of justice (Ps. 37:30).

The gates are open to me and I enter in, because I keep the truth (Isa. 26:2).

Justice will not be taken from me (Isa. 5:23).

I will not be destroyed with the wicked (Gen. 18:23).

I will go away into eternal life (Matt. 25:46).

My words are like choice silver (Prov. 10:20).

My words encourage many (Prov. 10:21).

My hope will be gladness (Prov. 10:28).

I will never be removed (Prov. 10:30).

My words bring forth wisdom (Prov. 10:31).

I am delivered through knowledge (Prov. 11:9).

I flourish like foliage (Prov. 11:28).

My roots yield fruit (Prov. 12:12).

The light in me rejoices and will not be put out (Prov. 13:9).

When I rejoice, there is great glory (Prov. 28:12).

I will see the fall of the wicked (Prov. 29:16).

I am glad and rejoice before God. Yes, I rejoice exceedingly (Ps. 68:3).

I will never be shaken. I will be in everlasting remembrance (Ps. 112:6).

I give thanks to Your name and dwell in Your presence (Ps. 140:13).

I will flourish like a palm tree. I will grow like a cedar in Lebanon (Ps. 92:12).

I eat to the satisfying of my soul (Prov. 13:25).

I will surely live and not sin, because I take the warning (Ezek. 3:21).

I speak what is acceptable (Prov. 10:32).

My fruit is a tree of life (Prov. 11:30).

I am rewarded here on earth (Prov. 11:31).

In my house there is much treasure (Prov. 15:6).

The name of the Lord is my strong tower. I run to it and am safe (Prov. 18:10).

My salvation is from the Lord. He is my strength in the time of trouble (Ps. 37:39).

It will be well with me, because I will eat the fruit of my doings (Isa. 3:10).

I will hold my way and will grow stronger and stronger (Job 17:9).

My words are a well of life (Prov. 10:11).

My desires will be granted (Prov. 10:24).

I have an everlasting foundation (Prov. 10:25).

I come through trouble and will not be ensnared (Prov. 12:13).

I think carefully before speaking (Prov. 15:28).

I will be glad in the Lord and will trust Him (Ps. 64:10).

I will flourish and live in an abundance of peace (Ps. 72:7).

My horns will be exhalted (Ps. 75:10).

My children will be delivered (Prov. 11:21).

The scepter of wickedness will not rest on the land allotted to me (Ps. 125:3).

I will not be forsaken, nor will my children beg for bread (Ps. 37:25).

I will shine forth like the sun in the kingdom of my Father (Matt. 13:43).

I do not walk according to the flesh but according to the Spirit (Rom. 8:4).

The ways of the Lord are right, and I walk in them (Hosea 14:9).

I am born of God, because I practice righteousness (1 John 2:29).

Riches and honor are with me, enduring riches and righteousness (Prov. 8:18).

The kingdom of heaven is mine, for I am persecuted for the sake of righteousness (Matt. 5:10).

I traverse the way of righteousness, in the midst of the paths of justice (Prov. 8:20).

The Lord loves me because I follow righteousness (Prov. 15:9).

PRAYERS OF THE RIGHTEOUS

Lord, do not allow my soul to famish, and do not cast away my desire (Prov. 10:3).

Lord, I cast my burden on You, and You will sustain me. You will not permit me to be moved (Ps. 55:22).

Lord, You have discerned that I am righteous and one who serves You. Make me Your jewel (Mal. 3:17–18).

Lord, let me be counted worthy of Your kingdom (2 Thess. 1:5).

Lord, bring my soul out of prison that I may praise Your name. Let the righteous surround me, for You will deal bountifully with me (Ps. 142:7).

Lord, let it be granted to me to be arrayed in fine linen, clean and bright (Rev. 19:8).

Lord, let the righteous requirement of the law be fulfilled in me (Rom. 8:4).

Let the wickedness of the wicked come to an end, but establish the just, for You, O God, test the heart and mind (Ps. 7:9).

Far be it from You, O Lord, to slay the righteous with the wicked. You, the Judge of all the earth, will do right (Gen. 18:25).

Hear in heaven, O Lord, and act, and judge Your servants, condemning the wicked, bringing his way on his head. Justify the righteous according to his righteousness (1 Kings 8:32).

I thank You, Lord, for the crown of righteousness that is laid up for me, for You will give it to me on that Day—and not just to me, but to all who have loved Your appearing (2 Tim. 4:8).

Let all the righteous blood shed on the earth from Abel to Zechariah come upon the heads of the scribes and Pharisees (Matt. 23:35).

Let the righteous strike me; it shall be a kindness. Let him rebuke me; it shall be as excellent oil; let my head not refuse it. For still my prayer is against the deeds of the wicked (Ps. 141:5).

Hear me when I call, O God of my righteousness (Ps. 4:1).

God is with the generation of the righteous. My enemies are in great fear (Ps. 14:5).

Because I practice righteousness, I am righteous, just as He is righteous (1 John 3:7).

Let the Lord reward me according to my righteousness, and according to the cleanliness of my hands may He reward me (2 Sam. 22:21).

Let me not trust in my own righteousness, despising others (Luke 18:9).

I hunger and thirst for righteousness. Lord, fill me (Matt. 5:6).

Lord, let me walk in the way of goodness and keep to the paths of righteousness (Prov. 2:20).

Let me not find treasures in wickedness, which profits me nothing, but let righteousness deliver me from death (Prov. 10:2).

Let blessings be upon my head (Prov. 10:6).

Let righteousness guard my way so that I will be found blameless (Prov. 13:6).

Let me be repaid with good (Prov. 13:21).

Let me not be reproached by sin but exhalted in righteousness (Prov. 14:34).

Let not my ways be an abomination unto the Lord (Prov. 15:9).

Lord, do not be far from me. Hear my prayer (Prov. 15:29).

The eyes of the Lord are on me, and His ears are open to my cry (Ps. 34:15).

Many are my afflictions, but Lord, You deliver me out of them all (Ps. 34:19).

Let light and gladness be sown for me (Ps. 97:11).

CHAPTER 3

THE PERSISTENT PRAYER

> Keep on asking, and you will receive what
> you ask for. Keep on seeking, and you will
> find. Keep on knocking, and the door will
> be opened to you.
>
> —MATTHEW 7:7, NLT

SOMETIMES ONCE ISN'T enough, and one prayer hasn't said it all or broken through. You find yourself praying again and again until you see the lines in the spirit begin to line up in your favor. This is called the persistent prayer. Persistence is another aspect of answered prayer. Persistence means not giving up. Persistence shows an earnest desire to receive an answer. This again reveals the condition of the heart. People who are not persistent lack the intensity that should be in the heart of righteous people.

Webster's Dictionary defines *persist* this way:

1. To go on resolutely or stubbornly in spite of opposition, importunity, or warning

2. To remain unchanged or fixed in a specified character, condition, or position

3. To be insistent in the repetition or pressing of an utterance (as a question or an opinion)

4. To continue to exist especially past a usual, expected, or normal time[1]

Synonyms for *persist* include to carry on, dig in, hang on, keep up, follow through with, knuckle down, abide, endure, hold on, hold up, last, remain, linger, stay, stick around, tarry, carry through, and prevail.[2] Persistence reveals an earnest desire to receive. Earnest means showing deep sincerity or seriousness, determined. Godly determination will be the force that drives people to pray without ceasing and be steadfast until the answer comes.

Does this sound like your prayer life? I know of many believers who get weary in prayer. They pray for a little while and get discouraged because the answer didn't come. The enemy never ceases to make war with the saints. He will never give up because His time is short. You must never cease praying.

The definition of *persist* also mirrors godly attributes. God persists and continues with us in our humanity. Jesus never ceases to make intercession for us (Isa. 53:12; Rom. 8:34). God is faithful. He sticks with us. He carries us through. When we pray persistent prayers, we are praying in the character of God.

The Continuing Prayer

Persist also means to continue past a usual or expected time. In the Bible there are many references to continuing prayer. This is also a prayer of persistence, of not giving up. Hannah is an example of one who continued in prayer to the point that the priest Eli thought she was drunk (1 Sam. 1:12–13). Hannah persisted until she got an answer—her son Samuel. In Acts 1 and 2 and throughout the forming of the early church the phrases "continued in prayer," "continued in prayer and supplication," "continued in faith, love, and holiness" are used to describe the apostles, who turned the world upside down with the gospel.

People who came to Jesus and continued with Him for days, coming before Him with their requests, were blessed, healed, delivered, and set free. Jesus had compassion on the multitude who had "continued" with Him for three days without food:

> Now Jesus called His disciples to Himself and said, "I have compassion on the multitude, because they have now continued with Me three days and have nothing to eat. And I do not want to send them away hungry, lest they faint on the way."
>
> —Matthew 15:32

Jesus was so moved by the people's hunger for spiritual food that He miraculously provided physical food for their bodies. They were seeking the things of the kingdom, and Jesus added the "all these things." Their persistence in seeking the Savior gave them the physical things they needed, and they weren't even praying for food.

In the verses before this creative miracle a Gentile woman came begging Jesus to deliver her demon-possessed daughter. Jesus did not answer her right away, but she persisted, even past the point of His seeming rudeness. She went even deeper with her request and bowed down in worship before Him. She was not giving up. She was willing to take even the crumbs from His table. She was willing, like the woman with the issue of blood, to just have a fragment of His healing virtue. She knew there was miracle power even in the leftovers of Jesus's presence. Jesus was amazed by her faith:

> "O woman, great is your faith! Let it be to you as you desire." And her daughter was healed from that very hour.
>
> —MATTHEW 15:28

Another example of persistence is found in Luke 18:35–40:

> Then it happened, as He was coming near Jericho, that a certain blind man sat by the road begging. And hearing a multitude passing by, he asked what it meant. So they told him that Jesus of Nazareth was passing by. And he cried out, saying, "Jesus, Son of David, have mercy on me!" Then those who went before warned him that he should be

quiet; but he cried out all the more, "Son of David, have mercy on me!" So Jesus stood still and commanded him to be brought to Him.

The people told this man to be quiet, don't bother Jesus. But this man was desperate. He was insistent on being heard so that Jesus could minister to him. His persistence resulted in his sight being restored.

James 5:11 says, "Behold, we count them happy which endure [continue, press, persist]. Ye have heard of the patience of Job, and have seen the end of the Lord; that the Lord is very pitiful, and of tender mercy" (kjv).

Some believers feel that we should not have to beg God to do anything for us. "If it's His will," many have said, "then He will just do it. We just need to believe." There may be times when this is true, but the people in the Bible who wanted a touch from Jesus did everything wrong according to the way the church people thought it needed to be done. They were loud. They were desperate. They were inappropriate. They cried out. They bowed low. They embarrassed themselves and others. They begged. They had mountains that needed to be moved, and they didn't care what was in the way of getting to Jesus. They just knew He was the One with the answer, and they did not give up asking and crying out to Him until they had their breakthrough.

PRAYING THROUGH

Believers who've been around for a while know this kind of persistence in prayer as tarrying or praying through. Smith Wigglesworth says:

> We ought not to stop until we pray through and receive our requests from God. We should prevail with God until we get a witness. Elijah prayed for rain and sent his servant seven times until he got the witness, which was a cloud the size of a man's hand. Then Elijah arose and went to tell Ahab that the rain was coming (1 Kings 18:42–44).
>
> Paul prayed thrice for a certain thing before God answered him (2 Cor. 12:8). God heard the first time, but Paul did not get the answer until he prayed three times.
>
> Oh, we should press or claim before the throne until we receive witness by the power of the Holy Ghost. God will do just what He promises.[3]

Some of the mountains in your life are so stubborn that they require you to PUSH—pray until something happens. Do not be discouraged. Press in. Remain. Endure. Hold on. Last. The Lord hears your prayers. Don't stop praying. Your breakthrough is near. Praying consistent, earnest prayers is part of the life of a believer who is doing something right. Continue in your position of prayer despite all apparent opposition. The enemy is only on the heels of those who recognize their strength and potential in God. Never give up praying about that lost loved one, that job, your finances, your health, your marriage, your church or ministry... Whatever it is, God is persisting with you. He has compassion on those who continue with Him.

PERSISTENT, EARNEST PRAYERS

I continue earnestly in prayer, being vigilant in it with thanksgiving (Col. 4:2).

I beg You earnestly, O God, do not send me away (Mark 5:10).

I earnestly seek You, God, and make my supplication to You, the Almighty (Job 8:5).

I earnestly desire the best gifts (1 Cor. 12:31).

I desire earnestly to prophesy and freely speak in tongues (1 Cor. 14:39).

I earnestly seek good; therefore, I will find favor (Prov. 11:27).

I seek earnestly for God (Ps. 78:34).

I groan, earnestly desiring to be clothed with the habitation of heaven (2 Cor. 5:2).

Like a servant, earnestly desiring shade, I too earnestly seek relief from my troubles (Job 7:2).

Lord, do not return to Your place. I acknowledge my offense and seek Your face. In my affliction I earnestly seek You (Hosea 5:15).

As I earnestly serve God day and night, I hope to attain the promise (Acts 26:7).

I earnestly obey Your commands, O Lord, to love You and serve You with all my heart and soul (Deut. 11:13).

I contend earnestly for the faith that was once for all delivered to the saints (Jude 3).

Like Elijah I will pray earnestly, and the rain will be subject to my prayers (James 5:17).

Lord, I hear You earnestly exhorting my fathers to obey Your voice. I will obey (Jer. 11:7).

Lord, I pray that as You earnestly remembered Ephraim, You would earnestly remember me. Let Your heart yearn for me and have mercy on me (Jer. 31:20).

As You did for Titus, put the same earnest care in my heart (2 Cor. 8:16).

I must give more earnest heed to the things I have heard, lest I drift away (Heb. 2:1).

Let the sons of God be revealed to meet creation's earnest expectation (Rom. 8:19).

Like Jesus, I am in agony. I will pray more earnestly (Luke 22:44).

Lord Jesus, I beg You earnestly to come and lay Your hands on my child that he (or she) may be healed and live (Mark 5:23).

According to my earnest expectation and hope that in nothing I will be ashamed, but with all boldness, as always, so now also Christ will be magnified in my body, whether by life or by death (Phil. 1:20).

Prayers That Continue

Lord, let my continual coming into Your presence cause You to avenge me (Luke 18:5).

Lord, I am one of those who have continued with You in Your trials (Luke 22:28).

Let brotherly love continue in my life (Heb. 13:1).

Lord, because You continue forever, You have an unchangeable priesthood (Heb. 7:24).

Like Hannah, I will continue praying before the Lord (1 Sam. 1:12).

I will begin to prosper and continue to prosper until I become very prosperous (Gen. 26:13).

I will give myself continually to prayer and to the ministry of the word (Acts 6:4).

I will rejoice in hope, be patient in tribulation, and continue steadfastly in prayer (Rom. 12:12).

I am continually in the temple praising and blessing God (Luke 24:53).

Lord, my sacrifices and burnt offerings are continually before You. Thank You, Lord, that You will not rebuke me (Ps. 50:8).

I will hope continually and will praise You yet more and more (Ps. 71:14).

You are continually with me, Lord. You hold me by my right hand (Ps. 73:23).

I will keep Your law continually, forever and ever (Ps. 119:44).

Like Daniel, I will continue in prayer and service (Dan. 1:21).

I will continue in faith, love, and holiness, with self-control (1 Tim. 2:15).

I will take heed to myself and to the doctrine. I will continue in them so that I may be saved (1 Tim. 4:16).

With the assembly I will continue to worship and sing until the burnt offerings are finished (2 Chron. 29:28).

I will wait on God continually. I will return and observe mercy and justice (Hosea 12:6).

I will continue in all the things that I have learned and been assured of, knowing from whom I have learned them (2 Tim. 3:14).

I will continue with one accord in prayer and supplication (Acts 1:14).

I will continue steadfastly in the apostles' doctrine and fellowship, in the breaking of bread, and in prayers (Acts 2:42).

With purpose of heart I will continue with the Lord (Acts 11:23).

Like Peter I will continue knocking until the door is opened (Acts 12:16).

Let the truth of the gospel continue with me (Gal. 2:5).

Let the flood waters recede continually from me. Let the flood waters decrease (Gen. 8:3).

I will continue in my work on the wall (Neh. 5:16).

Eternal life is granted to me, for by patient continuance in doing good, I seek for glory, honor, and immortality (Rom. 2:7).

Lord, have compassion on me as You did for the multitudes who continued with You and had nothing to eat (Mark 8:2).

I will remain and continue in the process and joy of faith (Phil. 1:25).

I will bless the Lord at all times; His praise shall continually be in my mouth (Ps. 34:1).

Continue, O God, Your lovingkindness to those who know You, and Your righteousness to the upright in heart (Ps. 36:10).

Hold me up, and I shall be safe, and I shall observe Your statutes continually (Ps. 119:117).

I will be blessed in what I do, because I look into the perfect law of liberty and continue in it. I am not a forgetful hearer but a doer of the work (James 1:25).

I am like a widow, left alone, but I trust in God and continue in supplications and prayers both night and day (1 Tim. 5:5).

Lord, I will continue in Your covenant with me. Do not disregard me as You did with the children of Israel whom You led by the hand out of the land of Egypt (Heb. 8:9).

I will continually offer the sacrifice of praise to God and the fruit of my lips, giving praise to His name (Heb. 13:15).

CHAPTER 4

THE PRAYER OF A CONTRITE HEART

The LORD is near to those who have a broken heart, and saves such as have a contrite spirit.

—PSALM 34:18

A BROKEN SPIRIT AND a contrite heart reveal repentance and godly sorrow. This again reveals the condition of the heart. Contrite means repentant, sorrowful, and regretful. God does not despise those who are contrite and broken; His compassion is revealed toward them. God's mercy is released on the behalf of the contrite. There are many prayers in the Bible asking for the mercy of God. God responds to the cries of those who are broken and asking for mercy. Healing, deliverance, and restoration are all the result of God's mercy. Praying for mercy is a powerful way to break through. The person requesting mercy is entirely dependent upon God.

For thus says the High and Lofty One who inhabits eternity, whose name is Holy: "I dwell in the high and holy place, with him who has a contrite and humble spirit, to revive the spirit of the humble, and to revive the heart of the contrite ones."

—ISAIAH 57:15

The Lord dwells with those who have a contrite or repentant heart. He hears their prayers and grants them grace because they are sorrowful and humble.

COMING AGAINST A PRIDEFUL SPIRIT— LEVIATHAN, KING OF PRIDE

Canst thou draw out leviathan with a hook? or his tongue with a cord which thou lettest down?...His scales are his pride, shut up together as with a close seal. One is so near to another, that no air can come between them....He beholdeth all high things: he is a king over all the children of pride.

—JOB 41:1, 15–16, 34, KJV

Leviathan is the personification of the spirit of pride. Pride is the opposite of the contrite, humble, and broken heart that God dwells with. God resists pride and turns His back on those who have given pride a place of authority in their lives. Those involved in the deliverance ministry will be familiar with Leviathan, the spirit of pride. You may be surprised when you encounter spirits that identify themselves as Leviathan. I am going to break down the character of this spirit so that you can get victory over it. This may be your mountain, or this may be why a mountain in your life has not been moved.

Leviathan's scales are his pride. No air can come between them. *Air* represents *spirit*, and one of the manifestations of pride is the inability to flow in the Spirit.

Leviathan will attempt to block the flow and manifestations of the Holy Spirit in the assembly. Proud people can hinder the flow of the Spirit. Humility is a key to operating in the power of the Holy Spirit. You need the power of the Holy Spirit to be able to break through the mountainous issues of life.

Leviathan protects himself with armor. Proud people have a way of closing themselves off and hiding behind the scales of pride. When attacking Leviathan, we attack and strip his scales.

> Will he make many supplications unto thee? will
> he speak soft words unto thee?
>
> —JOB 41:3, KJV

Supplication is prayer, and Leviathan does not make supplication because he is too proud. Leviathan will therefore attempt to block prayer and attack prayer ministries. We have also dealt with people who get sleepy when praying and found that it can be connected to Leviathan. This is why the spirit of pride must be broken down when you are facing tough circumstances in life. If you are not able to be persistent in your prayers or you don't have a desire to pray, you will not break through.

Leviathan does not speak soft words. Harsh words are another sign of Leviathan. He speaks roughly and does not speak with kindness.

> Will he make a covenant with thee? Wilt thou take him as a servant for ever?
>
> —JOB 41:4, KJV

Leviathan does not keep covenant. Leviathan is a covenant-breaking spirit. Many marriages have suffered because of the operation of Leviathan. A marriage will not survive if mates operate in pride and lack submission to one another. If you are facing impossible issues in your marriage, pride may be why. Covenant is also the key way through which believers receive the blessing and peace of God in their lives. Without covenant with God, there is no peace, prosperity, protection, and healing.

Leviathan does not serve. Pride will prevent us from serving one another. Serving is an act of humility, and Leviathan hates it.

> Wilt thou play with him as with a bird? or wilt thou bind him for thy maidens?
>
> —JOB 41:5, KJV

Don't play with pride. He is not a pet.

> Lay thine hand upon him, remember the battle, do no more.
>
> —JOB 41:8, KJV

The battle with pride may be one of the most difficult you will encounter. Pride is very strong in the lives of many, and it will take a fierce determination and persistence to defeat it.

> In his neck remaineth strength...
>
> —JOB 41:22, KJV

Leviathan is stiff-necked. Stubbornness and rebellion are signs of Leviathan. Israel was always called a stiff-necked people. God judged them for their stubbornness and rebellion.

> His heart is as firm as a stone; yea, as hard as a piece of the nether millstone.
>
> —JOB 41:24, KJV

Hardness of heart is another characteristic of Leviathan. It is also a root cause of divorce. (See Matthew 19:8.) Hardness of heart is connected to unbelief and the inability to understand and comprehend spiritual things.

> He maketh the deep to boil like a pot: he maketh the sea like a pot of ointment.
>
> —JOB 41:31, KJV

Leviathan dwells in the deep. Pride can be so deeply rooted in our lives and can be difficult to pull out. He is in the sea, which represents the nations. He causes the deep to boil and is responsible for restlessness.

> Thou brakest the heads of leviathan in pieces, and gavest him to be meat to the people inhabiting the wilderness.
>
> —PSALM 74:14, KJV

God has the power to smite and break Leviathan's head (authority). God is our King working salvation (deliverance) in the earth.

> I humbled my soul with fasting...
>
> —PSALM 35:13, KJV

Fasting is a great weapon against pride. When we fast, we humble our souls. We will talk more about the power combination of prayer and fasting in the last chapter.

Deliverance from Leviathan brings peace, favor, joy, and liberty. Pharaoh was a leviathan. God released His people from Pharaoh's grip through terrible judgments. The people left Egypt and journeyed to the Promised Land, a land flowing with milk and honey. Prosperity will come with deliverance from Leviathan.

Spirits of pride include arrogance, haughtiness, puffed up, self-exaltation, vanity, rebellion, stubbornness, scorning, defiance, anti-submissive, ego, perfection, Rahab, and Orion. Pride brings destruction. Pride brings a curse and causes a person to err (Ps. 119:21). God resists the proud (James 4:6). The fear of the Lord is to hate pride and arrogance (Prov. 8:13). God attempts to hide pride from man through dreams (Job 33:14–17). Sometimes sickness is the result of pride (vv. 17–26). Those who walk in pride, God is able to abase (Dan. 4:37).

51

Deliverance
Through Repentance

Pride causes rebellion and lack of repentance. Repentance shows humility and an openness to God's will being done. It shows a realization of His divine sovereignty and wisdom. Repentance is also a sign that the purpose and benefit of Christ's death have been received. When we repent, we take on the righteousness of Christ.

Sometimes the mountains of life are in your way because of unrepentant sin. You can have all the faith you want, worship and seek after God, but if you are not repenting and turning away from the sinful habits in your life, you could be making your way hard (Prov. 13:15). The good news is that if you confess your sin, God is faithful and just to forgive you of your sin and cleanse you from all unrighteousness (1 John 1:9).

Being able to speak to a mountain and have it move means that you are in right standing with God. The Bible says that the prayers of the righteous are powerful and effective (James 5:16). When you stand righteous and humble before God, believing in faith that He has heard you, you can have confidence that you will have what you have prayed.

Prayers for Mercy

Hear me when I call, O God of my righteousness: You enlarged me when I was in distress; have mercy on me, and hear my prayer (Ps. 4:1, kjv).

Have mercy upon me, O Lord; for I am weak: O Lord, heal me; for my bones are troubled (Ps. 6:2).

Have mercy upon me, O Lord; consider my trouble that I suffer from those who hate me. Lift me up from the gates of death (Ps. 9:13).

Hear, O Lord, when I cry with my voice: have mercy also upon me, and answer me (Ps. 27:7).

Hear, O Lord, and have mercy on me: Lord, be my helper (Ps. 30:10).

Have mercy on me, O Lord, for I am in trouble: my eye is consumed with grief, yes, my soul and my body (Ps. 31:9).

Have mercy on me, O God, according to Your loving-kindness: according to the multitude of Your tender mercies blot out my transgressions (Ps. 51:1).

Behold, as the eyes of servants look to the hand of their masters, and as the eyes of a maiden to the hand of her mistress; so my eyes wait on the Lord my God, until He has mercy on me (Ps. 123:2).

Jesus, Master, have mercy on me (Luke 17:13).

Jesus, son of David, have mercy on me (Luke 18:38).

I will not hold my peace, but I cry out to You all the more, "Son of David, have mercy on me" (Luke 18:39).

PRAYERS OF REPENTANCE

Lord, I repent in dust and ashes (Job 42:6).

I will repent so that I won't perish (Luke 13:3).

I repent for my wickedness and pray that the thoughts of my heart be forgiven me (Acts 8:22).

I will not tolerate the spirit of Jezebel in my life. I will not suffer anguish because of her adultery. I will repent and hold fast to what I have (Rev. 2:20–25).

Thank You, Lord, that my sins have been blotted out and times of refreshing have come from Your presence, because I have repented and been converted (Acts 3:19).

Lord, I repent. Do not remove my lampstand from its place (Rev. 2:5).

I receive the gift of the Holy Spirit, because I have repented and have been baptized (Acts 2:38).

Lord, I repent, for Your kingdom is at hand (Matt. 3:2).

Lord, I repent, that Your mighty works will be done in me (Matt. 11:20).

I will be zealous and repent because You love me and chasten me (Rev. 3:19).

I will turn to God and do the works befitting repentance (Acts 26:20).

I repent now for You will not always overlook my ignorance (Acts 17:30).

The Assyrian will not be my king, because I willingly repent (Hosea 11:5).

I repent and believe in the gospel (Mark 1:1).

I repent now of my evil way and evil doings that I may dwell in the land that the Lord has given to me and my fathers forever (Jer. 25:5).

I repent, Lord, and turn away from my idols and all my abominations (Ezek. 14:6).

Do not judge me, O Lord. I repent and turn from all my transgressions so that iniquity will not be my ruin (Ezek. 18:30).

I repent and make supplication to You, Lord, saying, "I have sinned and done wrong. I have committed wickedness" (1 Kings 8:47).

I remember what I have received and heard. I hold fast, repent, and remain watchful (Rev. 3:3).

Let repentance and remission of sins be preached in His name to all nations (Luke 24:47).

I repent before God and remain faithful toward my Lord Jesus Christ (Acts 20:21).

Godly sorrow produces repentance leading to salvation. I will not regret it (2 Cor. 7:10).

The Lord gives repentance to Israel and forgiveness of sins (Acts 5:31).

I will arise and go to my Father, and I will say to Him, "Father, I have sinned against heaven and before You" (Luke 15:18).

Prayers and Declarations of the Humble

Lord, I am humble. Guide me in justice and teach me Your ways (Ps. 25:9).

I will humble myself in the sight of the Lord, and He will lift me up (James 4:10).

I will not allow pride to enter my heart and cause me shame. I will be humble and clothed in wisdom (Prov. 11:2).

Lord, You take pleasure in me. You beautify me with salvation because I am humble (Ps. 149:4).

Lord, You will look on everyone who is proud, and You will humble them (Job 40:11).

Lord, You will save me (Ps. 18:27).

I will retain honor (Prov. 29:23).

I am better off being of a humble spirit with the lowly than dividing the spoil with the proud (Prov. 16:19).

I will humble myself under the mighty hand of God that He may exalt me in due time (1 Pet. 5:6).

My soul will make its boast in the Lord. The humble will hear of it and be glad (Ps. 34:2).

I will see what God has done and be glad. Because I seek God, my heart will live (Ps. 69:32).

I will not be like Amon, but I will humble myself before the Lord and will not trespass more and more (2 Chron. 33:23).

I will remove my turban and take off my crown and let nothing be the same. I will exalt the humble and humble the exalted (Ezek. 21:26).

I am in the midst of a meek and humble people, and they will trust in the name of the Lord (Zeph. 3:12).

I will increase my joy in the Lord. I will rejoice in the Holy One of Israel (Isa. 29:19).

Like Daniel, I will not fear, because I know that from the first day I set my heart to understand Your ways and to humble myself before You, You heard my words and have come to me (Dan. 10:12).

Lord, humble me and test me that I might do good in the end (Deut. 8:16).

I proclaim a fast right here that I might humble myself before my God, to seek from Him the right way for me and my children and all of my possessions (Ezra 8:21).

My God will humble me among His people and I will mourn for many who have sinned before and have not repented of the uncleanness, fornication, and lewdness that they have practiced (2 Cor. 12:21).

Lord, You said that if I humble myself, pray and seek Your face, and turn from my wicked ways, then You will hear from heaven and will forgive my sin and heal my land. Lord, I will do as You have commanded (2 Chron. 7:14).

Lord, You will dwell with him who has a contrite and humble spirit. You will revive the spirit of the humble and the hearts of the contrite ones. Let me be as they are (Isa. 57:15).

I will remember that the Lord my God led me all the way, even in the wilderness, to humble me and test me, to know what was in my heart, whether I would keep His commandments or not (Deut. 8:2).

God, You give more grace. You resist the proud but give grace to the humble (James 4:6).

Let me be like Moses, who was very humble, more than all the men who were on the face of the earth (Num. 12:3).

Lord, You do not forget the cry of the humble (Ps. 9:12).

Arise, O Lord! O God, lift up Your hand! Do not forget the humble (Ps. 10:12).

I will not set my mind on high things, but I will associate with the humble. I will not be wise in my own opinion (Rom. 12:16).

I will not pervert the way of the humble (Amos 2:7).

Lord, You have heard the desire of the humble; You will prepare their heart; You will cause Your ear to hear (Ps. 10:17).

I will submit myself to my elders. I will be clothed in humility, and God will give me grace (1 Pet. 5:5).

By humility and the fear of the Lord are riches, honor, and life (Prov. 22:4).

I will speak evil of no one. I will be peaceable and gentle, showing all humility to all men (Titus 3:2).

In humility I will correct those who are in opposition, and perhaps God will grant them repentance so that they may know the truth (2 Tim. 2:25).

The fear of the Lord is the instruction of wisdom, and before honor is humility (Prov. 15:33).

Before destruction the heart of a man is haughty, and before honor is humility (Prov. 18:12).

As the elect of God, holy and beloved, I will put on tender mercies, kindness, humility, meekness, and long-suffering (Col. 3:12).

I will seek the Lord. I will seek righteousness and humility so that I may be hidden in the day of the Lord's anger (Zeph. 2:3).

I take on the yoke of Christ, learning from Him, for He is meek and lowly in heart (Matt. 11:29).

I will do what the Lord requires of me: I will do justly, love mercy, and walk humbly with my God (Mic. 6:8).

I desire to be like Christ, who humbled Himself and became obedient to the point of death, even the death of the cross (Phil. 2:8).

Lord, I have humbled myself; please do not bring calamity upon me (1 Kings 21:29).

Through humility and the fear of the Lord I am given riches and honor and life (Prov. 22:4).

The Lord regards the lowly (Ps. 138:6).

I will humble myself as a little child (Matt. 18:4).

PRAYERS THAT BREAK A PRIDEFUL SPIRIT

May the Lord ruin the pride of Judah and the great pride of Jerusalem (Jer. 13:9).

I break the pride of Moab. It shall no longer be proud of its haughtiness, pride, and wrath. The lies it speaks will not be so (Isa. 16:6).

Thank You, Lord, that You turn me from my deeds and conceal my pride from me so that my soul may be kept back from the Pit and my life from perishing by the sword (Job 33:17).

Lord, I break the spirit of pride. Please answer when I cry out (Job 35:12).

I rebuke the shame that comes from a spirit of pride (Prov. 11:2).

I come against strife that comes with the spirit of pride (Prov. 13:10).

I break the spirit of pride, so that I will not fall and be destroyed (Prov. 16:18).

I break the spirit of pride. It will not bring me low. I will have a humble spirit (Prov. 29:23).

Pride will not serve as my necklace, nor will violence cover me like a garment (Ps. 73:6).

I will not be puffed up with pride and fall into the same condemnation as the devil (1 Tim. 3:6).

I break pride off of my life in the name of Jesus. I will not stumble in my iniquity like Israel, Ephraim, and Judah (Hosea 5:5).

The spirit of pride will not rule me. I shall not be desolate in the day of rebuke (Hosea 5:9).

The spirit of pride will not cause me to be scattered (Luke 1:51).

The Lord is above the spirit of the proud (Exod. 18:11).

Hear and give ear, spirit of pride. The Lord has spoken (Jer. 13:15).

The proud spirit of Ephraim and the inhabitant of Samaria will not speak (Isa. 9:9).

I command the spirit of pride to cease its persecution of the poor. Let that spirit be caught in the plots it has devised (Ps. 10:2).

Let not the foot of pride come against me, and let not the hand of the wicked drive me away (Ps. 36:11).

The Lord will cut off the pride of the Philistines (Zech. 9:6).

I break the pride of your power; I will make your heavens like iron and your earth like bronze (Lev. 26:19).

Let the pride of Moab be cut off at the root, for he is exceedingly proud of his loftiness, arrogance, pride, and the haughtiness of his heart (Jer. 48:29).

Let the pride of Israel be broken in the name of Jesus. Let them not testify to His face then go on not returning to the Lord their God (Hosea 7:10).

Lord, bring dishonor to the spirit of pride and bring into contempt all the honorable of the earth (Isa. 23:9).

I fear the Lord; therefore, I hate evil, pride, arrogance, and the evil way. I hate the perverse mouth (Prov. 8:13).

I break the spirit of the pride of life, for it is not of the Father but is of the world (1 John 2:16).

I will not be wise in my own eyes (Prov. 26:12).

Let the crown of pride, the drunkards of Ephraim, be trampled under foot (Isa. 28:3).

Like a swimmer reaches out to swim, Lord, spread out Your hands in their midst and bring down the prideful and their trickery (Isa. 25:11).

Like King Hezekiah, let prideful leaders humble themselves so that the wrath of the Lord does not come upon the people (2 Chron. 32:26).

Let not the pride of my heart deceive me. I have been brought low to the ground (Obad. 3).

Let the pride of the Jordan be brought to ruins (Zech. 11:3).

The proud in heart are an abomination to the Lord. Let them not go unpunished (Prov. 16:5)

The Lord abhors the pride of Jacob and hates his palaces. Let all their cities and everything in them be given to their enemies (Amos 6:8).

Those who walk in pride will be put down by the King of heaven (Dan. 4:37).

Those who uphold Egypt will fall; the pride of her power will come down, and those within her shall fall by the sword (Ezek. 30:6).

Let the pride of Assyria be brought down, and let the scepter of Egypt depart (Zech. 10:11).

Let those who rejoice in their pride be put to shame for any of their deeds. Let them be taken away. They shall no longer be haughty in My holy mountain (Zeph. 3:11).

I call the archers against the proud spirit of Babylon. Let all who bend the bow encamp against it all around. Let no one escape, for she has been proud against the Lord, the Holy One of Israel (Jer. 50:29).

I come against the spirit of the proud and haughty man who acts with arrogant pride (Prov. 21:24).

The Lord will bring down haughty looks (Ps. 18:27).

Let the king of Babylon be deposed from his kingly throne, for his heart is lifted up and his spirit is hardened in pride. Let his glory be taken away (Dan. 5:20).

I declare that this is the day that the Lord of hosts shall come upon everything proud and lofty, upon everything high and lifted up, and it shall be brought low (Isa. 2:12).

Let the most proud stumble and fall, and no one raise him up. Let the Lord kindle a fire in his cities, and it will devour all around him (Jer. 50:32).

I will let another man praise me, and not my own mouth; a stranger, and not my own lips (Prov. 27:2).

I dare not class myself or compare myself with those who commend themselves. They are not wise (2 Cor. 10:12).

I do not respect the proud or those who turn aside to lies. I make the Lord my trust (Ps. 40:4).

Lord, my heart is not haughty (Ps. 131:1).

Let the Lord halt the arrogance of the proud and lay low the haughtiness of the terrible (Isa. 13:11).

The Lord will not endure a haughty look and a proud heart (Ps. 101:5).

I will not talk proudly and will let no arrogance come from my mouth (1 Sam. 2:3).

The Lord resists the proud. Let me be like the humble one who receives grace from God (James 4:6).

The Lord will rise up a foreign army against the pride of the prince of Tyre. The most terrible of nations will draw their sword against the beauty of his wisdom. The Lord will defile the splendor of the proud spirit of the prince of Tyre, for his heart is lifted up declaring that he is a god. He will throw him in a pit, and he shall die the death of the slain. The Lord will break the spirit of the prince of Tyre, and he will no longer call himself a god, but a man, for he will die an outcast (Ezek. 28:2, 7–8).

I will not think of myself more highly than I ought to think. But I will remain sober minded (Rom. 12:3).

Let the prideful spirit of Haman be hanged on the gallows he prepared for God's chosen people (Esther 7:10).

I dismantle the scales of pride on the back of Leviathan (Job 41:15).

Let the rod of pride be broken in the mouth of a fool (Prov. 14:3).

Let Babylon, the glory of kingdoms and the beauty of the Chaldeans' pride, be overthrown as when God overthrew Sodom and Gomorrah (Isa. 13:19).

Let the wicked be taken in their pride and for the cursing and lying that they speak (Ps. 59:12).

The proud will not be blessed, and those who do wickedness will not be raised up. They will not tempt God and go free (Mal. 3:15).

I bridle my tongue so that it will not boast great things (James 3:5).

The Lord will bring down the haughty spirit (2 Sam. 22:28).

Let the proud and all who do wickedly become as stubble. Let neither root nor branch be left of them (Mal. 4:1).

I will not be broken off because of unbelief. I stand by faith. I will not be haughty, but I will fear (Rom. 11:20).

I will not boast about tomorrow, for I do not know what the day will bring forth (Prov. 27:1).

CHAPTER 5

THE PRAYER OF THE DESTITUTE

He shall regard the prayer of the destitute,
and shall not despise their prayer.
—PSALM 102:17

THE LORD HEARS the cry of His children when they are in need. It is His desire that none of us be in lack or in need. Psalm 102:17 says that He hears, looks upon, turns Himself toward, or holds in high regard the prayer of the destitute. Webster's dictionary defines *destitute* as "lacking something needed or desired; lacking possessions or resources; extreme poverty."[1] *Barnes' Notes* says *destitute* means:

> …"naked;" then, poor, stripped of everything, impoverished, wholly destitute. It would thus be eminently applicable to the poor exiles in Babylon; it is as applicable to sinners pleading with God, and to the people of God themselves, destitute of everything like self-righteousness, and feeling

that they have nothing in themselves, but that they are wholly dependent on the mercy of God.[2]

This can also refer to a spiritual state. Matthew 5:3 talks about the poor in spirit. That was every one of us before we were saved. Some of us, even though we are saved, still have lack in our lives. But the Bible says that God hears our prayers. He will not leave us naked, hungry, and without provision. He is the waymaker. It is in His Father nature to give good gifts to His children (Matt. 7:11). The second part of Matthew 5:3 says that He will give you the kingdom of heaven! The wealth and riches of the kingdom of heaven are far beyond your wildest imaginations.

Knowing the promises of God concerning you and your situation, you need to be strengthened in your spirit to pray against the things in your life that are not in line with what God has for you. Don't be so quick to settle in your state of destitution and lack, thinking this is your "lot" in life. No! You have the power to speak and pray against the work of the enemy when it comes to the provision you need for your physical and spiritual life. God said that He will not despise your prayers. He will not look down on them with contempt. He does not condemn you. On the contrary, He will come to your aid quickly. (See Revelation 22:12.) He will provide ways for you that are beyond the means of men. He says to you:

> Ho! Everyone who thirsts, come to the waters;
> and you who have no money, come, buy and eat.

> Yes, come, buy wine and milk without money and without price. Why do you spend money for what is not bread, and your wages for what does not satisfy? Listen carefully to Me, and eat what is good, and let your soul delight itself in abundance. Incline your ear, and come to Me. Hear, and your soul shall live.
>
> —Isaiah 55:1–3

He is a present help in your time of need. Your situation may seem hopeless, but God has already designed a way of escape. Do not get lost in your trouble. "Look up and lift up your heads, because your redemption draws near" (Luke 21:28). Speak to those mountains and tell them that your God will supply all your needs according to His riches in glory.

You Will Not Be Overcome

Problems can overwhelm you and give you the feeling of being swallowed up or overcome. *To be swallowed* means to be devoured, to perish, to be drowned or buried. At the end of this chapter I will give you prayers to reverse this and cause your problems to be swallowed instead. Demons are likened to serpents; all serpents are carnivorous, and nearly all seize and swallow living food (Jer. 51:34, NIV). Most snakes have specialized body structures that let them swallow things larger than their heads or necks. Don't allow the enemy to swallow your life, your finances, or your destiny. Rise up and pray for the Lord to swallow, consume, devour, overwhelm, and bury your problems instead. Synonyms for *swallow* include deplete, take back, exhaust, bury, engross, get down, swallow, accept, withdraw, finish, engulf, inhume, eat up, entomb, absorb, run through, immerse, swallow up, sink, eat, consume, lay to rest, soak up, wipe out, polish off, steep, plunge, inter, use up.

God swallowed Pharaoh and the Egyptians in the Red Sea. God opened the earth and swallowed Korah, Dathan, and Abiram. He will do the same to the evil that comes against you.

> The waters returned and covered the chariots, the horsemen, and all the army of Pharaoh that came into the sea after them. Not so much as one of them remained. But the children of Israel had walked on dry ground in the midst of the sea, and the waters were a wall to them on their right hand and on their left.
>
> —Exodus 14:28

> Who is like unto thee, O Lord, among the gods? who is like thee, glorious in holiness, fearful in praises, doing wonders? Thou stretchedst out thy right hand, the earth swallowed them.
>
> —Exodus 15:11–12, kjv

> Mine enemies would daily swallow me up: for they be many that fight against me, O thou most High.
>
> —Psalm 56:2, kjv

Thou shalt make them as a fiery oven in the time
of thine anger: the LORD shall swallow them up in
his wrath, and the fire shall devour them.

—PSALM 21:9, KJV

Do not let the floodwaters engulf me or the depths
swallow me up or the pit close its mouth over me.

—PSALM 69:15, NIV

THE CURSE OF
LUCK AND FORTUNE

Many of us have latched on to a worldly way of speaking
into our situations, saying this is good luck or that was
bad luck. I am not lucky or merely fortunate. I am blessed.
Fortunate means "favored by or involving good luck or
fortune; lucky. Auspicious or favorable." It is derived
from the pagan goddess Fortuna (equivalent to the Greek
goddess Tyche)—the goddess of fortune and personification of luck in Roman religion. She might bring good
luck or bad; she could be represented as veiled and blind,
as in modern depictions of justice, and came to represent life's unpredictability and inconsistence.[3] She was
also a goddess of fate. This definition of fortune takes it
further: "chance, luck as a force in human affairs"; "lot,
good fortune, misfortune"; "chance, fate, good luck"; or
"chance, luck."

> The Wheel of Fortune, or Rota Fortunae, is a
> concept in medieval and ancient philosophy refer-
> ring to the capricious nature of Fate. The wheel

belongs to the goddess Fortuna, who spins it at random, changing the positions of those on the wheel—some suffer great misfortune, others gain windfalls. Fortune appears on all paintings as a woman, sometimes blindfolded, "puppeteering" a wheel.[4]

Getting into the understanding of luck and fortune, we read in Isaiah 65:11–12 (AMP):

But you who forsake the Lord, who forget and ignore My holy Mount [Zion], who prepare a table for Gad [the Babylonian god of fortune] and who furnish mixed drinks for Meni [the god of destiny]—I will destine you [says the Lord] for the sword, and you shall all bow down to the slaughter, because when I called, you did not answer; when I spoke, you did not listen or obey. But you did what was evil in My eyes, and you chose that in which I did not delight.

Gad and Meni were the Pagan gods of fortune and destiny. Their names literally mean "troop" and "number." Gad is matched with Strong's H1408, but it is the same word as H1410, which means "troop." Meni is derived from *manah*, which means "to count, reckon, number, assign, tell, appoint, prepare." Isaiah 65:11 refers to the names of these two deities, Gad and Meni, but the thrust of the passage is that the Israelites had opted for polytheism ("that troop" and "that number") in defiance to their one God.[5]

We cannot be careless with what we use to describe the outcome of certain situations that occur in our lives. We can mistakenly be activating demonic deities to influence things that should be under God's authority.

When you turn your life over to God, you are not living by chance or the luck of the draw. You are living according to His divine plan. Jeremiah 29:11 says, "For I know the thoughts that I think toward you, says the LORD, thoughts of peace and not of evil, to give you a future and a hope." And the psalmist wrote in Psalm 37:23: "The steps of a good man are ordered by the LORD, and He delights in his way." Your life and the things you are going through are not spinning around randomly, and they are not out of control if you are in Christ. God is in control. Let your problems know this truth.

PRAYERS AGAINST CURSES AND BAD LUCK

I am not lucky; I am blessed.

In the name of Jesus, I rebuke all bad luck and bad fortune.

In the name of Jesus, I rebuke all gods and goddesses of fortune that would try to rule my life.

I repent and turn away from all superstition and belief in good luck.

In the name of Jesus, I rebuke and cast out all spirits of luck and good fortune.

In Jesus's name I renounce all items in my past associated with luck.

In the name of Jesus, I rebuke and cast out any demon trying to rule my destiny.

Lord, my destiny comes from You, and I will submit to Your plans and purposes for my life.

I declare that my steps are ordered by the Lord.

Lord, my future, success, and prosperity are in Your hands.

Prayers That Swallow the Enemy

Lord, You are the God that swallows Your enemies.

You swallowed Pharaoh in the Red Sea.

You swallowed Korah in the earth because of his rebellion.

You caused the earth to swallow the flood released by the dragon (Rev. 12:16).

You prepared a great fish to swallow up Jonah (Jon. 1:17).

Stretch out Your right hand, O God, and let the enemy (spiritual) be swallowed up.

In the name of Jesus, I rebuke the swallower.

Let the mouth of the swallower be closed and bound, in the name of Jesus.

Let all poverty and lack in my life be swallowed up, in the name of Jesus.

Let all sickness and disease be swallowed up.

Let all discouragement and defeat be swallowed up.

Let all assignments of hell against my life be swallowed up.

In Jesus's name, let all curses and negative words spoken against my life be swallowed up.

Let all Pharaohs who attempt to follow me be swallowed up.

The enemy will not be able to swallow my finances, but he must vomit them up (Job 20:15).

Punish the enemy, and let everything he has swallowed come forth, in the name of Jesus (Jer. 51:44).

My destiny and purpose will not be swallowed up by the enemy.

My life is preserved; it will not be swallowed up by the enemy.

My enemies will not swallow me up.

Let all the rods of the enemy be swallowed by the rod of God.

Let every Korah that rises against my life be swallowed up.

In the name of Jesus, let every generational stronghold be swallowed up.

Let all persecution against my life be swallowed up.

Fear, be swallowed up.

Witchcraft, be swallowed up.

Worry, be swallowed up.

Anxiety, be swallowed up.

Frustration, be swallowed up.

Everything that would attempt to swallow me, be swallowed up, in the name of Jesus.

Let every attack of hell against my life be swallowed up, in the name of Jesus.

I will not allow foolish words to swallow me up (Eccles. 10:12).

The Lord will send from heaven and deliver me from anything that would swallow me up (Ps. 57:3).

The water will not overflow me. The deep and the pit will not swallow me up (Ps. 69:15).

None of my belongings will be swallowed by wicked people (Luke 20:47).

Let all wickedness against me be swallowed up as Pharaoh and his host were swallowed up in the Red Sea, or as Korah, Dathan, and Abiram were swallowed up in the earth.

I rebuke and bind every serpent that tries to swallow anything belonging to me, in the name of Jesus.

In the name of Jesus, I bind and rebuke every python and constrictor that would attempt to squeeze and swallow.

I break the jaws of the wicked and pluck the spoil out of his teeth, so that he cannot swallow.

Lord, rebuke the devourer for my sake.

Let any problems that would overwhelm me be swallowed up, in the name of Jesus.

Send forth your mercy and truth, and deliver me from anything that would attempt to swallow me up (Ps. 57:3).

Hear me, O Lord; for Your lovingkindness is good: turn to me according to the multitude of Your tender mercies (Ps. 69:16).

What time I am afraid, I will trust in You (Ps. 56:3).

Let not the robber swallow up my substance (Job 5:5).

Lord, You are a God of wonders; let the powers of hell be swallowed up (Exod. 15:11–12).

Let anything that comes to eat up my flesh fall and be consumed (Ps. 27:2).

I release the dagger against all Eglons that come to swallow up the resources of God's people (Judg. 3:16–18).

I come against any wave of the enemy that would attempt to swallow me up.

Let not the waves overwhelm me (Ps. 93:3).

Let not the floods overwhelm and drown me.

Lord, You tread upon the waves (Job 9:8).

Lord, on high You are mightier than the noise of many waters, yes, than the mighty waves of the sea (Ps. 93:4).

Let the proud waves be stayed (Job 38:11).

You are the God that swallows death in victory.

Let all spirits of death and destruction be swallowed up.

Let spirits of the deep, the pit, and the abyss be swallowed up.

Let Abaddon and Appolyon be swallowed up.

Let all assignments of death and hell against my family be swallowed up, in the name of Jesus.

I refuse to be swallowed up with sorrow, for the joy of the Lord is my strength.

Let debt be swallowed from my life.

Let oppression be swallowed from my life.

Leap Prayers for Sudden Increase and Dramatic Advance*

I believe this is my appointed time to leap forward, in the name of Jesus.

It is my time to leap.

This is a new season of leaping for me.

I leap past all distractions, in the name of Jesus.

I leap past any people the enemy has set in my way to impede my progress.

Let my steps turn into leaps.

I leap over every wall erected by the enemy.

In the name of Jesus, I leap ahead of anyone or anything that has illegally jumped ahead of me.

I leap like a lion from Bashan like Dan.

I will leap over my enemies like David.

---

* These prayers are taken from Deut. 32:22; 2 Sam. 6:16; Ps. 18:29; Isa. 35:6; Luke 1:41; Luke 6:23; Acts 3:8; Acts 14:10.

I receive strength to leap out of all sickness and disease. I leap into my destiny and purpose, in the name of Jesus.

With excitement I leap into my future.

I leap from lack to abundance.

I leap from failure to success.

Let every place in my life that is lame leap for joy.

I take a leap of faith and do the impossible.

Let my finances grow by leaps and bounds.

Let my finances leap to a level I have not seen before.

Let wealth and prosperity leap upon my life, in the name of Jesus.

Let my wisdom increase by leaps and bounds.

Let my understanding increase by leaps and bounds.

Let my vision increase by leaps and bounds.

Let favor increase on my life by leaps and bounds.

Let my ministry grow by leaps and bounds.

Let my borders expand by leaps and bounds.

Let me leap and jump to the high places.

In the name of Jesus, let me catch up in any place I have fallen behind.

Let restoration come from anything stolen by the enemy from my life.

Let my revelation increase by leaps and bounds.

I will not be afraid to take a leap of faith at the word of the Lord.

I will leap upon the enemy and overwhelm him, in the name of Jesus.

I will leap and rejoice at the goodness of the Lord.

The Lord has given me leaping for sadness and joy for mourning.

I leap from a low place to a high place.

Let extra favor and blessing be added to my life, in the name of Jesus.

Let this year be a year of uncommon favor and blessing in my life.

Let me receive uncommon miracles and breakthroughs, in the name of Jesus.

Let me leap as a hart for joy.

I will leap into new places naturally and spiritually.

I will leap into new heights and levels.

I will leap above problems and setbacks, in the name of Jesus.

I will leap over all the traps and snares of the wicked one.

I break all chains and weights from my feet that would prevent me from leaping.

I lay aside every weight and burden that would prevent me from leaping.

I lay aside all doubt and unbelief that would keep me from leaping.

I leap from my past into my future.

I will not be afraid to leap forward with boldness and confidence.

I will leap for my God is with me.

My God encourages me and causes me to leap forward.

Let the kingdom advance in my city by leaps and bounds.

Let my timing and purpose be realigned this year, in the name of Jesus.

The way is opened for me, and I will leap into it.

I will join myself with other believers who are leaping forward.

Let the churches in my region leap forward.

Let our praise and worship leap to another level

Let my prayer life leap forward.

Let our preaching and teaching leap to another level.

I will leap forward in my giving.

Let my creativity leap to another level.

Let my faith take a quantum leap.

Let my love take a quantum leap.

Let my family leap forward into destiny.

Let my prophetic level take a quantum leap.

Let deliverance and healing take a quantum leap in my city, in the name of Jesus.

I will leap through fasting and prayer.

Let the blessings of the Lord overtake me and leap upon me, in the name of Jesus.

CHAPTER 6

MIDNIGHT AND MIDDAY PRAYER

Evening, and morning and at noon I will
pray, and cry aloud, and He shall hear my
voice.

—PSALM 55:17

PRAYING AT DIFFERENT times of the day can be a
powerful way to move mountains and experience
breakthroughs. I have always been a night person. I pray
and study at night. Understanding the mystery of the
night can cause you to see great breakthroughs in your
spiritual life.

Midnight prayer is a time for spiritual warfare. This
is the third watch of the night and one of the most
important times to keep watch. This is a special time
for divine government overruling human decrees! (See
Exodus 12–14.) This is when the deep sleep falls upon
men according to Acts 20:7–12. Remember, according
to Matthew 13:25, while men slept, the enemy went to
sow tares. This is therefore a period of heightened satanic

activities. The devil operates at this time because this is the time that men are sleep and there are not so many people praying to oppose him (1 Kings 3:20; Matt. 13:25).

> Night is also a time of anguish and fear for many, when pain, guilt, fear, and despair can seem almost unendurable. Many of the psalms call out to God from the depths of distress, for mercy, help, justice, victory over evil. Praying them, we give voice to the cries of the poor and troubled, those who are unable to turn to God themselves, or who do not even believe in God. We identify with those who are suffering, and call out with them and for them. Our prayer rises to God in the hours of darkness as an act of solidarity with those experiencing the night of the cross.[1]

In Psalm 42:8 we read, "The LORD will command His lovingkindness in the daytime, and in the night His song shall be with me—a prayer to the God of my life." According to *Adam Clarke's Commentary*, this verse is saying that God will give a special commission for His loving-kindness to visit us in the night hours, that He will allow His mercy to continue in our prayers, and give us power to make the best use of this visitation.[2]

That is a powerful revelation on the mystery of the night. When we pray at night, the Lord's love, kindness, and mercy will dwell in the midst of our prayers and be available to us in their full power. So if you are experiencing intense demonic opposition, the midnight hour would be an ideal place to establish a prayer post or vigil until you experience breakthrough.

BREAKTHROUGHS AT MIDNIGHT

The night has been established by covenant. Jeremiah 33:20 says, "Thus saith the LORD; If ye can break my covenant of the day, and my covenant of the night, and that there should not be day and night in their season" (KJV). Great breakthroughs can occur when we praise and pray at night. Midnight is a time when God does supernatural things. In Psalm 119:62 the psalmist said, "At midnight I will rise to give thanks unto thee because of thy righteous judgments" (KJV). Here is a list of other blessings or breakthroughs that occur at midnight.

Midnight is a time of release from every spiritual prison.

> And at *midnight* Paul and Silas prayed, and sang praises unto God: and the prisoners heard them.
> —ACTS 16:25, KJV, EMPHASIS ADDED

You can provoke God with fearful praises at midnight just as David and Paul did. It is a time of release from every spiritual prison; when you utilize the mystery of midnight prayers, it will initiate the earthquake of deliverance that would set you free.

> Then Moses said, "Thus says the LORD, 'About midnight I will go out into the midst of Egypt.'"
> —EXODUS 11:4

God's deliverance of Israel began at midnight.

> And it came to pass at midnight that the Lord struck all the firstborn in the land of Egypt, from the firstborn of Pharaoh who sat on his throne to the firstborn of the captive who was in the dungeon, and all the firstborn of livestock.
>
> —Exodus 12:29

Destruction of the enemy's gate happens at midnight.

> And Samson lay low till midnight; then he arose at midnight, took hold of the doors of the gate of the city and the two gateposts, pulled them up, bar and all, put them on his shoulders, and carried them up to the top of the hill that faces Hebron.
>
> —Judges 16:3

The bridegroom comes at midnight.

> Now it happened at midnight that the man [Boaz] was startled, and turned himself: and there, a woman [Ruth] was lying at his feet.
>
> —Ruth 3:8

> And at midnight a cry was heard: "Behold, the bridegroom is coming; go out to meet him!"
>
> —Matthew 25:6

Midnight is a time to ask.

> And He said unto them, "Which of you shall have a friend, and go to him at midnight and say to him, 'Friend, lend me three loaves.'"
>
> —LUKE 11:5

Catch the thief at midnight.

> And she arose at midnight, and took my son from beside me, while thine handmaid slept, and laid it in her bosom, and laid her dead child in my bosom.
>
> —1 KINGS 3:20, KJV

> You make darkness, and it is night, in which all the beasts of the forest creep about.
>
> —PSALM 104:20

God can instruct us at night.

> I will bless the LORD who has given me counsel: my heart also instructs me in the night seasons.
>
> —PSALM 16:7

God can visit us at night.

> You have tested my heart; You have visited me in the night; You have tried me and have found nothing; I have purposed that my mouth shall not transgress.
>
> —PSALM 17:3

We can meditate on God and the Word at night.

> When I remember You on my bed, I meditate on
> You in the night watches.
>
> —Psalm 63:6

> My eyes are awake through the night watches,
> that I might meditate on Your word.
>
> —Psalm 119:148

It is good to desire God in the night.

> With my soul I have desired You in the night, yes,
> by my spirit within me I will seek You early; for
> when Your judgments are in the earth, the inhab-
> itants of the world will learn righteousness.
>
> —Isaiah 26:9

**Nehemiah could see the desolation of the broken
walls of the city at night.**

> So I went up in the night by the valley, and viewed
> the wall; then I turned back and entered by the
> Valley Gate, and so returned.
>
> —Nehemiah 2:15

The Lord appeared to Solomon at night.

> Then the Lord appeared to Solomon by night,
> and said to him, "I have heard your prayer, and
> have chosen this place for Myself as a house of
> sacrifice."
>
> —2 Chronicles 7:12

Nicodemus sought Jesus at night.

> Nicodemus (he who came to Jesus by night, being one of them)...
>
> —John 7:50

Angels of deliverance can come at night.

> But at night an angel of the Lord opened the prison doors and brought them out.
>
> —Acts 5:19

> For there stood by me this night an angel of the God to whom I belong and whom I serve.
>
> —Acts 27:23

Destroying the Works of Darkness

When the king of Syria came to arrest Elisha in 2 Kings 6:13–14, he came in the night. For the kingdom of darkness, nighttime is conference time. It is when the enemies meet to deliver their reports, re-strategize and take decisions concerning the fate of many—including Christians. It is also when they renew covenants, curses, and sacrifices. It is the time they supervise the burdens, punishment, and yokes already placed on their victims. But more importantly, it is the time they alter the destiny of many. Every night activity of the satanic kingdom against you this season will come to nothing in Jesus's name.

Believers must be active participants in the spiritual realm. Praying for one hour at night has great effects on the operations of the dark kingdom, much more all night prayer. Reduce your sleep! As they meet to determine your fate, you go on your knees and determine theirs, scatter their meeting and strip them powerless.[3]

Midnight is also the witching hour, the time of day when supernatural creatures such as witches, demons, and ghosts are thought to appear and be at their most powerful, and black magic at its most effective. This hour is typically past midnight or the time in the middle of the night when magic things are said to happen.

> At midnight I will rise to give thanks to You, because of Your righteous judgments.
>
> —Psalm 119:62

In Psalm 91:6 the psalmist mentions the pestilence that walks in darkness: "Nor of the pestilence that walks in darkness, nor of the destruction that lays waste at noonday." This is a picture of evil walking at night.

Midnight speaks of darkness—the absence of light and the presence of blindness. It is for rest and is unsuitable for labor. It is favorable to the purposes of wickedness. Wild beasts seek their prey at night. Shepherds watch over their sheep at night. The midnight is a period of severe calamities. Darkness has binding powers and limits activities. It has separating powers. That is when all that is evil and unworthy of light is let loose. But the enemy does not own the night; the night belongs to God: "The day is Yours, the *night* also is Yours; You have prepared the light and the sun" (Ps. 74:16, emphasis added).

Mark 1:35 tells us that Jesus prayed at night: "And in the morning, rising up a great while before day, he went out, and departed into a solitary place, and there prayed" (KJV). He is our example of how to stay connected to God, free from unbelief, and remain in the power of the supernatural and miracles.

Midnight is a great and strategic time to pray. Midnight represents the darkness of the night. Night is symbolic of darkness and the time when men are sleeping. The enemy likes to plan and work when men are sleeping, so rising up at night in prayer will definitely thwart and interrupt his plans.

MIDDAY PRAYER

The whole idea of praying at 12:00 p.m. (midday) is that it allows God to interrupt your day. Whether or not you already have a regular time of prayer, disciplining yourself to pray in the center of your day means your mind returns to God regardless of the pressures or busyness of daily life.

> Nor of the pestilence that walks in darkness, nor of the destruction that lays waste at noonday.
> —PSALM 91:6

There is also an opportunity to pray against the midday curse. Deuteronomy 28:29 says that "at midday you will grope about like a blind man in the dark. You will be unsuccessful in everything you do; day after day you will be oppressed and robbed, with no one to rescue you" (NIV). This is the plan of the enemy at work. We can establish a defense against this vicious plan by seeking God and praying against the enemy at noon.

Noon is the high point of the day and the sun. The sun is responsible for warmth and prosperity. "High noon" is defined as the most advanced, flourishing, or creative stage or period. *High* means "elevated above any starting point of measurement, as a line, or surface; having altitude; lifted up; raised or extended in the direction of the zenith; lofty; tall; as, a high mountain, tower, tree; the sun is high." Synonyms for *high noon* include:

> acme, apex, apogee, brow, cap, climax, cloud nine, crest, crown, culmen, culmination, edge, eight bells, extreme limit, extremity, heaven, heavens, height, highest pitch, highest point, limit, maximum, meridian, meridiem, midday, mountaintop, ne plus ultra, no place higher, noon, noonday, nooning, noonlight, noontide, noon-time, peak, pinnacle, pitch, point, pole, ridge, seventh heaven, sky, spire, summit, tip, tip-top, top, upmost, upper extremity, uppermost, utmost, vertex, very top, zenith.[4]

Noon prophetically represents a high point. Pray high things at noon. Pray to be lifted higher in the things of God and the Spirit.

PRAYERS TO RELEASE THE MORNING AND THE DAYSPRING

Lord, You command the morning and cause the dayspring to know his place. Let all wickedness be shaken out of my life, in the name of Jesus (Job 38:12–13).

Let the morning and the dayspring arise in my life.

Let the dew of the morning be upon my life, in the name of Jesus.

Let the blessing of the morning arise in my life, in the name of Jesus.

Let the Sun of righteousness arise with healing in his wings, and let every area of my life be healed, in the name of Jesus.

Lord, You are a sun and a shield for my life. Withhold no good thing from my life.

With this new morning let new mercy and favor be upon my life, in the name of Jesus.

Jesus, You are my Dayspring; release more light and revelation into my life.

Dayspring, take Your place in my life.

Dayspring from on high, visit me.

Let wickedness be shaken out of my family, city, region, and nation, in the name of Jesus.

Let the wicked scatter as the dayspring takes his place.

Dayspring, take hold of the ends of the earth and root out wickedness.

Dayspring, take hold of the ends of the earth and drive out darkness.

Nothing is hidden from You, Lord, for You created the dayspring.

Let there be a new dawning in my life, in the name of Jesus.

I praise You, Lord, in the morning.

Let Your name be praised from the rising of the sun to the going down of the same (Ps. 113:3).

PRAYERS TO RELEASE THE MERCY AND FAVOR OF THE MORNING

Cause me to hear Your lovingkindness in the morning; for in You do I trust. Cause me to know the way that I should walk, for I lift up my soul to You (Ps. 143:8).

I will sing of Your power; yes, I will sing aloud of Your mercy in the morning. You have been my defense and refuge in the day of my trouble (Ps. 59:16).

Show forth Your lovingkindness in the morning and Your faithfulness every night (Ps. 92:2).

Because of Your mercy, Lord, I am not consumed. Your compassions never fail. They are new every morning. Great is Your faithfulness (Lam. 3:22–23).

Lord, You are my sun and shield. You give me grace and glory and will withhold no good thing from me (Ps. 84:11).

Lord, You are a sun and shield; let my life be protected by You in the day and the night.

Prayers to Release the Blessing of High Noon

Let the blessing of the sun be upon my life.

Let me experience a great and joyful harvest, in the name of Jesus (Deut. 33:14).

Lord, the day is Yours and the night also. You have prepared the light and the sun (Ps. 74:16).

The Lord God is my strength. He will make my feet like hinds' feet and will make me to walk on my high places (Hab. 3:19).

Also now, behold, my witness is in heaven, and my record is on high (Job 16:19).

The Lord is my rock, fortress, and deliverer; He is my God, my strength, in whom I will trust. He is my buckler, the horn of my salvation, and my high tower (Ps. 18:2).

He makes my feet like the feet of deer and sets me on my high places (Ps. 18:33).

From the end of the earth I will cry to You, when my heart is overwhelmed; lead me to the rock that is higher than I (Ps. 61:2).

I am poor and sorrowful; let Your salvation, O God, set me up on high (Ps. 69:29).

The Highest Himself shall establish me (Ps. 87:5).

I dwell in the secret place of the Most High and abide under the shadow of the Almighty (Ps. 91:1).

Because I have set my love upon Him, He will deliver me; He will set me on high because I have known His name (Ps. 91:14).

He has set me on high from affliction and makes my family like a flock (Ps. 107:41).

I will dwell on high; my place of defense shall be the fortress of rocks. Bread shall be given me, and my waters shall be sure (Isa. 33:16).

A highway will be there for me—a way—and it shall be called the way of holiness. The unclean will not pass over it, but I will walk along this highway and will not go astray (Isa. 35:8).

I will get up into the high mountain. I will lift my voice and say to the cities, "Behold your God" (Isa. 40:9).

The Lord will open to me the rivers in high places and fountains in the midst of the valleys. He will make the wilderness a pool of water and the dry land springs of water (Isa. 41:18).

I will feed along the road, and my pasture will be in all high places (Isa. 49:9).

God will make my mountains a road, and my highways will be elevated (Isa. 49:11).

Lord, I surrender to Your ways; for as the heavens are higher than the earth, so are Your ways higher than mine and Your thoughts than my thoughts (Isa. 55:9).

PRAYERS TO REDEEM FROM THE CURSE AT MIDDAY

I am redeemed from the curse at midday (Deut. 28:29).

I am redeemed from destruction at midday (Ps. 91:6).

I will praise and pray at midday (Ps. 55:17).

The sun will not smite me by day (Ps. 121:6).

The sun will bless my life. My life will be fruitful (Deut. 33:13–16).

I will not be vain or vexed under the sun (Eccles. 1:14).

I will love and enjoy life under the sun (Eccles. 2:17)

I will not be oppressed under the sun; I have the Comforter—the Holy Spirit (Eccles. 4:1).

DECLARATIONS AGAINST THE OPERATION OF EVIL AT NIGHT

I bind and rebuke anything operating against me at night, in the name of Jesus.

I will not be tormented at night.

Anything operating under the cover of darkness, be exposed, in the name of Jesus.

Darkness will not overwhelm my life, but I have the light of life.

I will not be afraid of the terror at night.

Let every prison door be opened, and let every foundation of wickedness be shaken.

Lord, release Your angels of deliverance for me, in the name of Jesus.

The day and the night belong to You, Lord; let me be blessed in the day and the night.

You created the day and the night for Your pleasure, Lord. Let me enjoy the day and the night.

CHAPTER 7

PRAYER AND FASTING

> Then the disciples came to Jesus privately
> and said, "Why could we not cast him
> out?" So Jesus said to them, "Because of
> your unbelief; for assuredly, I say to you, if
> you have faith as a mustard seed, you will
> say to this mountain, 'Move from here to
> there,' and it will move; and nothing will be
> impossible for you. However, this kind does
> not go out except by prayer and fasting."
>
> —MATTHEW 17:19–21

UNBELIEF IS AN enemy to overcoming mountains of
what seems to be impossible. In Matthew 13:58 we
find that Jesus did not operate in the power of God in
His hometown because of the unbelief of the people. The
disciples could not cast out a strong demon because of
unbelief.

It is important to drive unbelief from your life. And
one of the ways this is accomplished is through prayer
and fasting. Prayer and fasting help us clear obstacles to
our faith and faith-filled actions.

Fasting, coupled with prayer, is one of the most powerful weapons to receiving a breakthrough and overcoming unbelief. Jesus preceded His ministry with fasting and returned in the power of the Spirit into Galilee. Jesus did not struggle with unbelief, and He operated in faith throughout His ministry. When you are challenged with unbelief in any situation, I encourage you to fast and pray for breakthrough.

FASTING RELEASES THE BREAKER ANOINTING

What are your mountains? In the introduction I named many of the common mountains we all face at different seasons in our lives. Maybe you've been praying over these things for a long time and have not seen breakthrough.

In Micah 2:13 the prophet prophesied, "The one who breaks open will come up before them; they will break out, pass through the gate, and go out by it; their king will pass before them, with the LORD at their head." We are living in the days of the breaker. The Lord is the breaker. He is able to break through any obstacle, opposition, or mountain on behalf of His people. There is a breaker anointing arising upon the church. We will see and experience more breakthroughs than ever before.

Fasting is one of the ways to increase the breaker anointing. Fasting will cause breakthroughs in families, cities, nations, finances, church growth, salvation, healing, and deliverance. Fasting will help you to break through the toughest situations. Fasting will help you to break through all opposition of the enemy.

There are some spirits in a person, region, or nation that cannot be overcome without fasting. Many believers struggle with certain limitations they cannot seem to break through. A revelation of fasting will change this and result in victories that would not be ordinarily obtained. A life of consistent fasting will cause many victories to manifest. God's will is that every believer live a life of victory with nothing being impossible.

There are stubborn spirits that will respond only to fasting and prayer. These tend to be generational strongholds that tenaciously hold on to families and nations for years. Fasting will break these strongholds. These strongholds include poverty, sickness, witchcraft, sexual impurity, pride, fear, confusion, and marital problems. Do any of these sound like the mountains you are facing today? Fasting will help you overcome these strongholds and break free from their limitations.

> But you, when you fast, anoint your head and wash your face, so that you do not appear to men to be fasting, but to your Father who is in the secret place; and your Father who sees in secret will reward you openly.
>
> —MATTHEW 6:17–18

Fasting breaks the mountain of the spirit of poverty (Joel 2:15, 18-19).

Joel gave the people of Israel the proper response to the locust invasion. Locusts represent demons that devour. Locusts represent the spirits of poverty and lack. The locust had come upon Israel and devoured the harvest. Joel encouraged the people to fast and repent. God promised to hear their prayer and answer by sending corn, wine, and oil.

Corn, wine, and oil represent prosperity. Fasting breaks the spirit of poverty and releases the spirit of prosperity. I have seen countless numbers of believers struggle in the area of their finances. Prosperity is elusive to many. This mountain of poverty can be moved through fasting and prayer.

Fasting breaks the mountain of fear and releases great things (Joel 2:21).

Do you desire to see great things happen in your life? The Lord desires to do great things for His people. Fasting prepares the way for great things to happen. These great things include signs and wonders.

Fasting causes us to become more fruitful (Joel 2:22).

Fasting increases the fruit of a believer's life. This includes the fruit of the Spirit. God desires His people to be more fruitful. Fasting helps our ministries become more fruitful.

Fasting releases the rain (Joel 2:23).

Rain represents the outpouring of the Holy Spirit. Rain also represents blessing and refreshing. Israel needed the former rain to moisten the ground for planting. They needed the latter rain to bring the crops to maturity. God has promised to give the former and latter rains in response to fasting.

Fasting moistens the ground (the heart) for the planting of the seed (the Word of God). Fasting causes the rain to fall in dry places. Nations and cities that have not experienced revival can receive rain through fasting.

Fasting releases the Holy Spirit and increases the prophetic anointing (Joel 2:28).

Fasting helps to release one of the greatest promises given by the prophet Joel. This is the promise of the last-day outpouring of the Holy Spirit. Fasting helps to release the manifestation of prophecy. Fasting also helps release visions and dreams.

Fasting breaks the mountain of sexual impurity (Judg. 19:22–20:5).

Sexual sin is one of the hardest sins to break. Many believers struggle with generational lust. Lust spirits cause much shame, guilt, and condemnation. This robs the believer of the confidence and boldness he should have. Many believers struggle with masturbation, pornography, perversion, and fornication. Fasting will help drive these spirits from a person's life.

Fasting brings enlargement and deliverance (Esther 4:14–16).

Fasting was a part of defeating Haman's plans to destroy the Jews. The whole nation of Israel was delivered because of fasting. Esther needed favor from the king and received it as a result of fasting. Fasting releases favor and brings great deliverance.

The Jews not only defeated their enemies, but they were also enlarged. Mordecai was promoted and Haman was hung. Enlargement comes through fasting. Fasting breaks limitations and gives you more room to expand and grow. God desires to enlarge our borders (Deut. 12:20). God wants us to have more territory. This includes natural and spiritual territory. Fasting breaks limitations and causes expansion.

Fasting breaks the mountain of sickness and infirmity and releases healing (Isa. 58:5–6, 8).

Many believers struggle with sicknesses such as cancer, diabetes, high blood pressure, sinus problems, and chronic pain. These spirits of infirmity are often generational. Fasting helps eliminate chronic sicknesses and diseases. God has promised that our health will spring forth speedily.

Fasting releases God's glory for our protection (Isa. 58:8).

Divine protection is another promise from Isaiah 58. God promises to protect us with His glory. Fasting releases the glory of the Lord that covers us. God has promised to cover the church with glory as a defense (Isa. 4:5). The enemy cannot penetrate or overcome this glory.

Fasting results in answered prayer (Isa. 58:9).

Demonic interference causes many prayers to be hindered. Daniel fasted twenty-one days to break through demonic resistance and receive answers to his prayers. The prince of Persia withstood the answers for twenty-one days. Daniel's fast helped an angel to break through and bring the answers.

Fasting will cause many answers to prayer to be accelerated. These include prayers for salvation of loved ones and deliverance. Fasting helps to break the frustration of unanswered prayer.

Fasting releases divine guidance (Isa. 58:11).

Many believers have difficulty making correct decisions concerning relationships, finances, and ministry. This causes setbacks and wasted time because of foolish decisions. Fasting will help believers make correct decisions by releasing divine guidance. Fasting eliminates confusion. Fasting causes clarity and releases understanding and wisdom to make correct decisions.

Fasting is recommended for those who are making important decisions such as marriage and ministry choices.

Fasting breaks generational mountains and curses (Isa. 58:12).

Many of the obstacles that believers encounter are generational. Generational curses result from the iniquity of the fathers. Generational sins such as pride, rebellion, idolatry, witchcraft, occult involvement, Masonry, and lust open the door for evil spirits to operate in families through generations. Demons of destruction, failure, poverty, infirmity, lust, and addiction are major strongholds in the lives of millions of people.

Fasting helps loose the bands of wickedness. Fasting lets the oppressed go free. Fasting helps us to rebuild the old waste places. Fasting reverses the desolation that results from sin and rebellion.

Fasting closes the breaches and brings forth restoration (Isa. 58:12).

There are many believers who need restoration. They need restoration in their families, finances, relationships, health, and walk with the Lord. Fasting is a part of restoration.

Fasting closes the breaches. Breaches are gaps in the wall that give the enemy an entry point into our lives. Breaches need to be repaired and closed. When the breaches are closed, the enemy no longer has an opening to attack.

Fasting restores the ancient paths (Isa. 58:12).

Fasting helps keep us on the right path. Fasting helps to prevent us from going astray. Fasting will help those who have strayed from the right path to return. Fasting is a cure for backsliding. Fasting will help restore us to the right path.

Fasting helps us to walk in the good path (Prov. 2:9),

the path of life (v. 19), the path of peace (Prov. 3:17), the old path (Jer. 6:16), and the straight path (Heb. 12:13). Fasting restores these paths and helps us to walk in them.

Fasting causes you to have great victory against overwhelming odds (2 Chron. 20:3).

Jehoshaphat was facing the combined armies of Moab, Ammon, and Edom. He was facing overwhelming odds. Fasting helped him to defeat these enemies. Fasting helps us to have victory in the midst of defeat.

Jehoshaphat called a fast because he was afraid. Fear is another stronghold that many believers have difficulty overcoming. Fasting will break the power of the demon of fear. Spirits of terror, panic, fright, apprehension, and timidity can be overcome through fasting. Freedom from fear is a requirement to live a victorious lifestyle.

Fasting prepares the way for you and your children and delivers you from enemies that lie in wait (Ezra 8:21, 31).

Ezra fasted because he recognized the danger of his mission. Fasting will protect you and your children from the plans of the enemy. Fasting will stop the ambush of the enemy. Fasting will cause your substance to be protected from the attack of the enemy.

Fasting breaks the mountains of pride, rebellion, and witchcraft (Ps. 35:13; Job 33:17–20).

Sickness can be the result of pride. Pain can also be the result of pride. Sickness often results in the loss of appetite. This is a forced fast. Fasting humbles the soul.

Fasting helps us overcome the strongman of pride. Pride and rebellion are generational spirits that are often difficult to overcome.

Gluttony and drunkenness are signs of rebellion (Deut. 21:20). Rebellion is as the sin of witchcraft (1 Sam. 15:23). God humbled Israel in the wilderness by feeding them with only manna (Deut. 8:3). Israel lusted for meat in the wilderness. This was a manifestation of rebellion (Ps. 106:14–15).

Fasting causes the joy and presence of the Lord to return (Mark 2:20).

The presence of the bridegroom causes joy. Weddings are filled with joy and celebration. When a believer loses the joy and presence of the Lord, he or she needs to fast. Fasting causes the joy and presence of the Lord to return. No believer can live a victorious life without the presence of the Bridegroom.

Fasting releases the power of the Holy Spirit for the miraculous (Luke 4:14, 18).

Fasting increases the anointing and the power of the Holy Spirit in a person's life. Jesus ministered in power after fasting. He healed the sick and cast out devils. All believers are expected to do the same works (John 14:12). Fasting helps us to walk in the power of God. Fasting releases the anointing for miracles.

Fasting Must Be Genuine, Not Religious or Hypocritical

In Luke 18:11–12 the Pharisee fasted with attitudes of pride and superiority. These attitudes are not acceptable to God. God requires humility and sincerity in fasting. We must have the correct motives in fasting. Fasting is a powerful tool if done correctly. Fasting cannot be done religiously or hypocritically.

Isaiah 58 describes the fast that God had chosen. Fasting cannot be done with amusement (v. 3). Fasting cannot be done while mistreating others (v. 3). Fasting cannot be done for strife and contention (v. 4). Fasting causes one to bow his head like a bulrush (v. 5). Fasting must be done in humility. Fasting is a time of searching the heart and repenting. Fasting must be done in an attitude of compassion for the lost and hurting (v. 7). This is the fast that God promises to bless.

The enemy knows the power of prayer and fasting, and he will do everything in his power to stop you. Believers who begin to fast can expect much spiritual resistance. You must be committed to a fasted lifestyle. The rewards of fasting far outweigh the obstacles of the enemy. A revelation of the power of fasting will help you to break through!

PRAYERS AGAINST STUBBORN DEMONS AND STRONGHOLDS*

I bind, rebuke, and cast out every stubborn demon that would attempt to stubbornly hold on to my life in the name of Jesus.

I come against every stubborn stronghold and command it to yield to the power of God and the name of Jesus (2 Sam. 5:7).

I put pressure on every stubborn demon and stronghold and break its grip in my life, in the name of Jesus.

I uproot every stubborn root from my life, in the name of Jesus (Matt. 15:13).

I command every stubborn, ironlike yoke to shatter and break, in the name of Jesus (Judg. 1:19).

I break the power of every proud, stubborn, and arrogant demon that exalts itself against Christ, and I command it to be abased, in the name of Jesus.

In the name of Jesus, I break the power of all iniquity in my family that would stubbornly attempt to control my life.

I come against all obstinate demons, and break their influence in my life in the name of Jesus.

---

* These prayers coupled with fasting and deliverance will bring break-through (Matt. 17:21).

I rebuke all stubborn, habitual patterns of failure and frustration in my life in the name of Jesus.

I rebuke all stubborn pharaohs that would attempt to hold God's people, and I command you to let God's people go, in the name of Jesus (Exod. 8:32).

In the name of Jesus, I bind and rebuke all stubborn enemies, who stubbornly oppose me and my progress.

I rebuke all stubborn demons that would attempt to resist the power of God and the authority I have through Jesus Christ, and I render you powerless to resist, in the name of Jesus.

I come against every persistent pattern that limits me, and I render it powerless against me, in the name of Jesus.

There is nothing impossible through faith. I release my faith against every stubborn and obstinate demon, and I resist you steadfastly, in the name of Jesus (Matt. 19:26).

I weaken, break down, and pressure every stubborn demon and stronghold; you are getting weaker and weaker, and I am getting stronger and stronger.

I exercise long war against all stubborn demons until you are completely defeated and destroyed from my life, in the name of Jesus (2 Sam. 3:1).

I lay siege against every stubborn stronghold through prayer and fasting, until your walls come down, in the name of Jesus (Deut. 20:19).

I use the battering ram of prayer and fasting to demolish all the gates of every stubborn stronghold, in the name of Jesus.

Let every Jericho wall fall through my praise, as I lift my voice as a trumpet against you, in the name of Jesus (Josh. 6:1, 20).

Let every demonic stump be removed from my life, in the name of Jesus.

In the name of Jesus, I break the will of every stubborn spirit that would attempt to remain in my life.

I speak to every stubborn demon: You have no will to remain, your will is broken, and you must submit to the name of Jesus and the power of the Holy Ghost.

I come against all stubborn demons and strongholds in my family that have refused to leave, and in the name of Jesus, I assault every demonic fortress that has been built for generations.

I rebuke every stubborn mule and bull of Bashan from my life, in the name of Jesus.

In the name of Jesus, I break the will of every stubborn mule that comes against me. You are defeated and must bow to the name above all names (Ps. 22:12).

The anointing is increasing in my life through prayer and fasting, and every stubborn yoke is being destroyed (Isa. 10:27).

NOTES

CHAPTER 1
THE PRAYER OF FAITH

1. Larry Keefauver, ed., *The Original John G. Lake Devotional* (Lake Mary, FL: Charisma House, 1997), 149.

2. Ibid., 149–150.

3. Larry Keefauver, ed., *The Original Azusa Street Devotional* (Lake Mary, FL: Charisma House, 1997), 119–120.

4. Kenneth E. Hagin, "Gift of Faith and the Working of Miracles," cFaith.com, http://www.cfaith.com/index .php?option=com_content&view=article&id=1171:gift-of -faith-and-the-working-of-miracles&catid=45:faith&Itemid=91 (accessed March 14, 2012).

CHAPTER 3
THE PERSISTENT PRAYER

1. Merriam-Webster.com, Dictionary, s.v. "persist," http://www .merriam-webster.com/dictionary/persist (accessed April 17, 2012).

2. Merriam-Webster.com, Thesaurus, s.v. "persist," http://www .merriam-webster.com/thesaurus/persist (accessed April 17, 2012).

3. Keefauver, ed., *The Original Azusa Street Devotional*, 102.

CHAPTER 5
THE PRAYER OF THE DESTITUTE

1. Merriam-Webster.com, Dictionary, s.v. "destitute,"http://www .merriam-webster.com/dictionary/destitute (accessed April 18, 2012).

2. *Barnes' Notes*, electronic database, s.v. "Ps. 102:17," PC Study Bible, copyright © 1997 Biblesoft.

3. Webster's Online Dictionary, s.v. "Common Expressions: Fortuna," http://www.websters-online-dictionary.org/definitions /Fortuna?cx=partner-pub-0939450753529744%3Av0qd01 -tdlq&cof=FORID%3A9&ie=UTF-8&q=Fortuna&sa=Search#906 (accessed April 18, 2012).

4. Wikipedia.org, s.v. "Rota Fortunae," http://en.wikipedia.org /wiki/The_Wheel_of_Fortune_(medieval) (accessed April 18, 2012).

5. KJVToday.com, "'Troop/Number' or 'Fortune (Gad)/Destiny (Meni)" in Isaiah 55:11?", http://www.kjvtoday.com/home/ troopnumber-or-fortune-gaddestiny-meni-in-isaiah-6511 (acessed April 18, 2012).

CHAPTER 6
MIDNIGHT AND MIDDAY PRAYER

1. Sr. Eleanor, "Vigils: Prayer During the Darkness of Night," *Cistercian Vocation* (blog), June 22, 2008, http:// cistercianvocation.wordpress.com/2008/06/22/vigils-prayer -during-the-darkness-of-night/ (accessed April 18, 2012).

2. *Adam Clarke's Commentary*, electronic database, s.v. "Psalms 42:8," PC Study Bible, copyright © 1996 Biblesoft.

3. Pasor E. Adeboye, "Night Vigil," SolidRockDublin.org, February 22, 2011, http://solidrockdublin.org/?p=1417 (accessed March 27, 2012).

4. *Moby Thesaurus*, s.v. "high noon," Babylon.com, http:// thesaurus.babylon.com/high%20noon (accessed April 19, 2012).

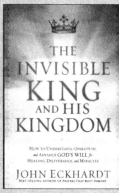
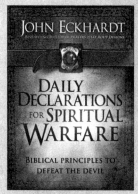

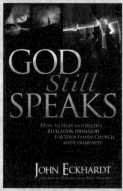

BOOK 1

PRAYERS that RELEASE HEAVEN on EARTH

JOHN ECKHARDT

CHARISMA
HOUSE

HAIL TO THE LORD'S ANOINTED

1. Hail to the Lord's Anointed,
Great David's greater Son!
Hail, in the time appointed,
His reign on Earth begun!
He comes to break oppression,
To set the captive free,
To take away transgression,
And rule in equity.

2. He comes with succor speedy
To those who suffer wrong;
To help the poor and needy,
And bid the weak be strong;
To give them songs for sighing,
Their darkness turn to light,
Whose souls, condemned and dying,
Were precious in His sight.

3. He shall come down like showers
Upon the fruitful earth;
And love, joy, hope, like flowers,
Spring in His path to birth.
Before Him on the mountains

Shall peace, the herald, go;
And righteousness, in fountains,
From hill to valley flow.

4. Arabia's desert ranger
To Him shall bow the knee;
The Ethiopian stranger
His glory come to see;
With offerings of devotion
Ships from the isles shall meet,
To pour the wealth of ocean
In tribute at His feet.

5. For Him shall prayer unceasing
And daily vows ascend;
His kingdom still increasing,
A kingdom without end.
The tide of time shall never
His covenant remove;
His name shall stand forever;
That name to us is Love.

6. The heav'ns which now conceal Him,
In counsels deep and wise,
In glory shall reveal Him
To our rejoicing eyes;
He who, with hands uplifted,

When from the earth below,
Shall come again all gifted,
His blessings to bestow.

7. Kings shall fall down before Him,
And gold and incense bring,
All nations shall adore Him,
His praise the people sing.
Outstretched His wide dominion,
O'er river, sea and shore,
Far as eagle's pinion,
Or dove's light wing can soar.

8. O'er every foe victorious,
He on His throne shall rest;
From age to age more glorious,
All-blessing and all-blest.
The tide of time shall never
His covenant remove;
His name shall stand for ever,
His changeless name of Love.*

    —James Montgomery

---

* "Hail to the Lord's Anointed," words by James Montgomery, a paraphrase of Psalm 72, written December 1821, published 1822. Public domain.

CONTENTS

INTRODUCTION

GOD HAS A marvelous plan for His church, a plan that will help release heaven on the earth. The prophets predicted a time when salvation, righteousness, peace, joy, rejoicing, and redemption will come to Israel and the world. Jerusalem (Zion) will be restored and once again become the dwelling place of God. The heathen (nations) will come to the God of Israel and worship. It will be a time of the establishing of an everlasting covenant (new covenant). God's plans are for a time when old things (former things) pass away and new things spring forth. There will be an outpouring of the Holy Spirit and the release of living waters from Jerusalem, which will flow to the nations.

It is time for God's people to get on board with God's plan and to diligently pray—and work—to see the fulfillment of God's plan for His church.

God has given us a clear mandate for what we should be doing. He says:

> If My people who are called by My name will humble themselves, and pray and seek My face, and turn from their wicked ways, then I will hear from heaven, and will forgive their sin and heal their land.
> —2 Chronicles 7:14

I have written this book for you to understand thoroughly that God's plan is to establish and advance His kingdom. As you read, may your heart be stirred with a longing for the fulfillment of God's plan to release heaven on the earth. Be filled with hope for an earth filled with His righteousness. See how God's plan is unveiled in the pages of the Gospels. Get excited to challenge yourself to diligently pray for God's plan—God's kingdom, heaven—to be released on Earth *now*.

In Section II of this book you will find hundreds of prayers and decrees that will help you to keep your mind and heart focused on the plan of God.

Use the words of Isaiah as your call to others: "Of the increase of His government and peace there will be no end, upon the throne of David and over His kingdom, to order it and establish it with judgment and justice from that time forward, even forever. The zeal of the Lord of hosts will perform this" (Isa. 9:7).

SECTION 1

UNDERSTANDING GOD'S PLAN

CHAPTER 1

GOD'S PLAN FOR
A KINGDOM

THE ESTABLISHMENT OF the kingdom of God included the restoration of the tabernacle of David (Acts 15) with the coming of the Gentiles into the church. The righteous will flourish, and the earth will be filled with the knowledge of the Lord. God plans to accomplish all of this through the Messiah-King, His Son, Jesus Christ.

During Bible times, the prophets saw the coming kingdom as a time of great joy and rejoicing. They prophesied that everlasting joy would be upon the head of the righteous, and they would obtain gladness and joy (Isa. 35:10; 51:11). Zion would be the joy of many generations (Isa. 60:15). Those who believe the gospel would receive the oil of joy

(Isa. 61:1–3), and they would receive everlasting joy (v. 7).

The Lord would cause rejoicing to fill Jerusalem and to fill her people with joy (Isa. 65:19). This indicates new-covenant Jerusalem, the church (Heb. 12:22). The nations would be glad and sing for joy because of the rule of Messiah (Ps. 67:4). Mount Zion (the church) rejoices (Ps. 48:11).

Israel had never experienced earthly peace for any extended period of time. The peace they desire would come only through Messiah, and it would be spiritual. The peace they needed was hidden from their eyes, and it was prophesied that they would experience a Roman invasion (Luke 19:41–44). They were looking for an earthly peace and missed the spiritual peace that comes through Christ. *Peace* is the Hebrew word *shalom*, meaning "prosperity, health, wholeness."

Jesus is the Prince of Peace (Isa. 9:6). The increase of His government and peace will have no end (v. 7). The gospel is called the *gospel of peace* (Rom. 10:15). Fulfillment of the kingdom of God began to come to the nations because of the preaching of the gospel. Today the preaching of the gospel is still taking place, and as believers we can usher in God's kingdom plan through our prayers. Those who preach the gospel publish peace, which is part of the plan of God for His kingdom (Isa. 52:7; Nah. 1:15). The new covenant is the covenant of peace (Isa. 54:10; Ezek. 34:25; 37:26), and the prayers of believers fulfill the plan of God and expand the peace of God.

The prophets spoke of the coming kingdom in terms of peace. The King would bring peace to the people (Ps. 72:3), and the righteous would have an abundance of peace (v. 7). The Lord would ordain peace for His people (Isa. 26:12). The work of righteousness would be peace (Isa. 32:17). The kingdom of peace would come through the suffering of the Messiah. The chastisement of our peace was upon Him (Isa. 53:5). We are led forth with peace (Isa. 55:12). God would extend peace like a river (Isa. 66:12). He would speak peace to the heathen (Zech. 9:10).

It is God's plan that righteousness would reign in His kingdom. The Old Testament is filled with references to the righteousness of the kingdom. In the New Testament, we learn that we are made the righteousness of God in Christ (2 Cor. 5:21). He is our righteousness (1 Cor. 1:30). Israel could not attain righteousness through the Law. Righteousness comes through faith and the new covenant. Today, as believers in Christ and His righteousness, we are living in the kingdom. The Christian—the new man—is created in righteousness and true holiness (Eph. 4:24). Yet we have not yet experienced a world filled with peace and righteousness. As we pray these prayers, we can expect righteousness, peace, and joy to increase from generation to generation.

CHAPTER 2

GOD'S PLAN WILL RELEASE HEAVEN ON EARTH

THE ANNOUNCEMENT OF the nearness of the kingdom was an announcement of the coming righteousness of the kingdom. This righteousness would come through the gospel (Rom. 1:17). The righteousness of the kingdom could not come by the Law, but through faith in the Messiah. God's plan will not take place through worldly things (meat and drink). His plan is for a spiritual kingdom, one that is filled with His righteousness.

The Jews were looking for an earthly kingdom and missed the righteousness that comes by faith. Many missed the kingdom and the righteousness that comes through faith in the gospel. Today, many people—including Christians—are still not seeing God's plan fulfilled because they are looking at earthly solutions for God's spiritual kingdom. We must strengthen our faith in God's power to usher in His kingdom and pray diligently for His plan to be unfolded.

The prophets spoke of the coming righteousness of the kingdom. The kingdom is connected to the gospel (Isa. 52:7). The righteousness of God would come to Israel and the nations through the gospel. Many in Israel missed the kingdom because they did not obey the gospel (Rom. 10:15–16). They did not submit to the gospel. They did not submit to the righteousness of God (v. 3). They became enemies of the gospel and therefore enemies of the kingdom (Rom. 11:28; 1 Thess. 2:14–16).

Today we must pray earnestly for righteousness to come to our homes, our communities, our nation, and our world. We must pray that the world's rampant disobedience to the plans and will of God will cease. We must pray for people to turn in obedience to God! Pray that the righteousness of

God will come to the nations of the world and to the homes of people throughout our world.

We learn in Isaiah 32:17 that the work of righteousness will be demonstrated in peace (*shalom*), and that the work of righteousness will demonstrate quietness and confidence. As we pray in quietness and confidence for this to happen today, our prayers will include these characteristics of God's plan:

- Righteousness will be revealed (Isa. 56:1).
- The saints will be called trees of righteousness (Isa. 61:3).
- Righteousness and praise will spring forth among the nations (Isa. 61:11).
- The Messiah will bring in everlasting righteousness (Dan. 9:24).
- The new man—new believers—will be created in righteousness (Eph. 4:24).
- The new covenant will administrate righteousness (2 Cor. 3:9).
- The scepter of the kingdom will be righteousness (Heb. 1:8).

- The righteous will flourish in the days of the Messiah (the kingdom—Ps. 72:7).

How marvelous it will be when the plans of God for His kingdom can permeate every corner of this world. The Bible tells us that "the righteous will be planted in the land" (Isa. 60:21). Can you imagine the time when America has so many righteous believers "planted" throughout its regions that our entire nation is known in today's world as a righteous land?

Unfortunately, today America is recognized throughout the world as a nation that is straying away from its righteous foundations. Instead of righteousness filling our streets, we have rebellion against God, and wickedness and sin that are terrifying the people of America. If the people of America—and of the nations—are to be recognized as the planting of the Lord, we must pray for God to have mercy on our rebelliousness and sinfulness and to call us to repentance. America must turn back to the godly foundations upon which it was birthed. As you read these pages, commit to praying diligently for the plans of God to be fulfilled in America and throughout the world so that the plan of God and the kingdom of God can be established.

We will become the planting of the Lord only as we place our faith and trust in the gospel (Isa. 61:1–3). An earthly kingdom requires an earthly land, but a spiritual kingdom does not. We must recognize that we are praying for a spiritual kingdom. The Bible tells us that Abraham was not looking for an earthly land but a heavenly country (Heb. 11:14–16). We must be seeking a heavenly America today.

It is God's plan to fill the world with righteousness. The Old Testament is filled with references to the righteousness of the kingdom. We are made the righteousness of God in Christ (2 Cor. 5:21). Christ is our righteousness (1 Cor. 1:30). Israel could not attain righteousness through the Law. Righteousness comes through faith and the new covenant. We are now living in the kingdom and the new covenant.

As you pray, thank God that He has fulfilled His plan through Christ, His Son. Include the following promises in your prayers.

PRAYERS

Lord, we pray that "all the mighty ones upon earth…shall come and shall declare His righteousness to a people yet to be born—that He has done it [that it is finished]!" (Ps. 22:29, 31, AMP).

Lord, may I be able to say, "I have proclaimed glad tidings of righteousness in the great congregation; behold, I will not restrain my lips, O LORD, You know. I have not hidden Your righteousness within my heart; I have spoken of Your faithfulness and Your salvation; I have not concealed Your lovingkindness and Your truth from the great congregation" (Ps. 40:9–10, NAS).

Lord, "let the heavens declare His righteousness, for God Himself is Judge" (Ps. 50:6).

Lord, "my adversaries are all before You [fully known to You]....Let one [unforgiven] perverseness and iniquity accumulate upon another for them [in Your book], and let them not come into Your righteousness or be justified and acquitted by You. Let them be blotted out of the book of the living and the book of life and not be enrolled among the [uncompromisingly] righteous (those upright and in right standing with God)" (Ps. 69:19, 27–28, AMP).

Father, "my mouth shall tell of Your righteousness and Your salvation all the day, for I do not know their limits. I will go in the strength of the Lord GOD; I will make mention of Your righteousness, of Yours only" (Ps. 71:15–16).

"Your righteousness reaches to the skies, O God, you who have done great things. Who, O God, is like you?" (Ps. 71:19, NIV).

Father, I pray that the prayer of Solomon will be true in the nations today: "Give the gift of wise rule to the king, O God, the gift of just rule to the crown prince. May he judge your people rightly, be honorable to your meek and lowly....Please stand up for the poor, help the children of the needy, come down hard on the cruel tyrants....Let righteousness burst into blossom and peace abound until the moon fades to nothing. Rule from sea to sea" (Ps. 72:1–8, The Message).

Lord, my prayer will continually rise to You until our nation reflects Your Word, which promises: "Love and faithfulness meet together; righteousness and peace kiss each other. Faithfulness springs forth from the earth, and righteousness looks down from heaven....Righteousness goes before him and prepares the way for his steps" (Ps. 85:10–11, 13, niv).

Father, "blessed are those who have learned to acclaim you, who walk in the light of your presence, O Lord. They rejoice in your name all day long; they exult in your righteousness. For you are their glory and strength" (Ps. 89:15–17, niv).

Father, hear our prayers for the nations, that "the LORD will not reject his people; he will never forsake his inheritance. Judgment will again be founded on righteousness, and all the upright in heart will follow it" (Ps. 94:14–15, NIV).

"The LORD reigns, let the earth be glad; let the distant shores rejoice....The heavens proclaim his righteousness, and all the peoples see his glory" (Ps. 97:1, 6, NIV).

Lord, I praise You because Your Word has promised: "The LORD has made his salvation known and revealed his righteousness to the nations. He has remembered his love and his faithfulness to the house of Israel; all the ends of the earth have seen the salvation of our God" (Ps. 98:2–3, NIV).

Father, I praise You because "from everlasting to everlasting the LORD's love is with those who fear him, and his righteousness with their children's children" (Ps. 103:17, NIV).

Lord, with the psalmist, I will declare, "Praise the LORD. I will extol the LORD with all my heart in the council of the upright and in the assembly. Great are the works of the LORD; they are pondered by all who delight in them. Glorious and majestic are his deeds, and his righteousness endures forever" (Ps. 111:1–3, NIV).

Father, this is the prayer of my heart: "Open for me the gates of righteousness; I will enter and give thanks to the LORD. This is the gate of the LORD through which the righteous may enter. I will give you thanks, for you answered me; you have become my salvation" (Ps. 118:19–21, NIV).

CHAPTER 3

GOD'S PLAN IS REVEALED THROUGH THE GOSPEL

THE KINGDOM IS a mystery. The joining of Jew and Gentile in the church is a mystery (Eph. 3:1–6). It has been given unto us to know the mysteries of the kingdom (Mark 4:11). The plan of God was to establish His kingdom through the church; when this is done, heaven will be released on the earth. The church made known to the principalities and powers the manifold wisdom of God (Eph. 3:10). The kingdom was the eternal purpose of God in Christ (v. 11).

Jesus Christ (the Anointed One) is the key to the fulfillment of these kingdom promises. Jesus was anointed to bring the message of the kingdom and to establish the kingdom. We are now living

21

in the days of the Messiah-King. We can enjoy the blessings of the kingdom and pray for the kingdom to advance. Of the increase of His government (kingdom) and peace (*shalom*) there will be no end. The kingdom is from generation to generation. Our prayers and decrees help advance the kingdom in our generation and prepare the way for generations to come.

The kingdom of God is connected to the gospel. To preach the gospel is to preach the kingdom. When Jesus walked on earth, He proclaimed: "The time is fulfilled, and the kingdom of God is at hand. Repent, and believe in the gospel" (Mark 1:15).

The gospel is a declaration of the reign of God.

> How beautiful upon the mountains
> Are the feet of him who brings good news,
> Who proclaims peace,
> Who brings glad tidings of good things,
> Who proclaims salvation,
> Who says to Zion,
> "Your God reigns!"
>
> —Isaiah 52:7

God's Plan Is Revealed Through the Gospel

It is God's plan to reign over the heathen through the preaching of the gospel. "God reigns over the nations; God sits on His holy throne" (Ps. 47:8). The reign of God is a heavenly, spiritual reign over the nations. It is not a physical or geographical reign. There is no substitute for the preaching of the gospel.

The gospel of the kingdom is the gospel of peace. The enemies of the gospel are the enemies of the kingdom. They are also the enemies of peace. But God has proclaimed, "How beautiful are the feet of those who bring glad tidings! [How welcome is the coming of those who preach the good news of His good things!]" (Rom. 10:15, AMP).

The gospel of the kingdom is also the gospel of Christ. To preach Christ is to preach the kingdom. To submit to Christ is to submit to the kingdom. The gospel was preached to Abraham. Through his seed would all the families of the earth be blessed. This is fulfilled through Christ and the gospel. And today, the plan of God is that the nations will be justified through faith in Jesus Christ.

> The Scripture foresaw that God would
> justify the Gentiles by faith, and announced
> the gospel in advance to Abraham: "All
> nations will be blessed through you."
> —Galatians 3:8, NIV

The kingdom is a mystery, and so is the gospel. When we pray for the mysteries of God to be revealed, we are praying for the mystery of the kingdom to be revealed. The apostle Paul prayed:

> Pray also for me, that whenever I open my
> mouth, words may be given me so that I
> will fearlessly make known the mystery of
> the gospel.
> —Ephesians 6:19, NIV

God's plan—God's kingdom, the release of heaven on earth—is revealed through the gospel:

> Now to him who is able to establish you
> by my gospel and the proclamation of
> Jesus Christ, according to the revelation of
> the mystery hidden for long ages past, but

now revealed and made known through
the prophetic writings by the command of
the eternal God, so that all nations might
believe and obey him.

> —Romans 16:25–26, NIV

We pray that the word of the Lord would have free course. This is praying for the kingdom to advance.

message of the Lord may spread rapidly
and be honored, just as it was with you.

Finally, brothers, pray for us that the
message of the Lord may spread rapidly
and be honored, just as it was with you.

> —2 Thessalonians 3:1, NIV

CHAPTER 4

GOD'S PLAN FOR THE GENTILES

I T IS THE plan of God that the kingdom of God have dominion over the Gentiles. "He shall have dominion also from sea to sea, and from the River to the ends of the earth" (Ps. 72:8).

Israel had the promise of the nations being subdued under them. "For the LORD Most High is awesome; He is a great King over all the earth. He will subdue the peoples under us, and the nations under our feet" (Ps. 47:2–3).

This plan would come to pass through Messiah. Many in Israel viewed this promise as a physical dominion over the Gentiles. The rule over the Gentiles through Christ was being fulfilled in the first century (Rom. 15:8–12). It is fulfilled through

Christ and the church. The Gentiles were coming
into the tabernacle of David (Acts 15:15–17). The
tabernacle of David was the rule of Christ, the son
of David. There is, however, no physical dominion
of Israel over the Gentiles. The kingdom is not
physical, but spiritual.

The nations were being subdued through the
gospel. The gospel was to the Jew first. The nations
were being saved through the Jewish Messiah. The
dominion was spiritual. The nations were coming
under the reign of Christ in fulfillment of Isaiah
11:10. Israel's glory would be the salvation of the
Gentiles (Isa. 60).

Many in Israel missed this glory because they
were expecting a worldly kingdom instead of a
heavenly kingdom. Instead of rejoicing in the
salvation of the nations, many in Israel opposed the
gospel. The nations were being subdued to Israel
through their Messiah, yet many missed it because
they were looking for a kingdom with observation
(Luke 17:20–21). The Gentiles were submitting to
the kingdom through the gospel.

Israel never subdued their enemies for any extended period of time. They usually were under Gentile dominion. Military conquest would not be the fulfillment of dominion promises. Christ would subdue the nations through the gospel of peace. The kingdom is not advanced through the sword but through preaching.

Christ did subdue the enemies of the kingdom, and there are references to warfare in the Book of Revelation. The enemies of the kingdom were the first-century generation that opposed the gospel and persecuted the church. Christ subdued the nations through the gospel, and He subdued His enemies through judgment.

The following old covenant promises are fulfilled in Christ:

> All the ends of the world
> Shall remember and turn to the LORD,
> And all the families of the nations
> Shall worship before You.
> For the kingdom is the LORD's,

And He rules over the nations.
>   —Psalm 22:27–28

I will praise You, O Lord, among the peoples;
I will sing to You among the nations.
>   —Psalm 57:9

That Your way may be known on earth,
Your salvation among all nations.
>   —Psalm 67:2

Oh, let the nations be glad and sing for joy!
>   —Psalm 67:4

Yes, all kings shall fall down before Him;
All nations shall serve Him.
>   —Psalm 72:11

All nations shall call Him blessed.
>   —Psalm 72:17

Arise, O God, judge the earth;
For You shall inherit all nations.
>   —Psalm 82:8

All nations whom You have made
Shall come and worship before You, O
    Lord,
And shall glorify Your name.

—Psalm 86:9

I will praise You, O LORD, among the
    peoples,
And I will sing praises to You among the
    nations.

—Psalm 108:3

Praise the LORD, all you Gentiles!
Laud Him, all you peoples!

—Psalm 117:1

These scriptures could never be completely fulfilled under the old covenant. The heathen (nations) were in darkness. They were "aliens from the commonwealth of Israel and strangers from the covenants of promise, having no hope and without God in the world" (Eph. 2:12). These scriptures can be fulfilled only in Christ, through the church, under the new covenant, in the present kingdom age.

Praise and worship among the nations are the manifestation of the kingdom. The Gentiles would glorify God for His mercy.

> And that the Gentiles might glorify God for His mercy, as it is written:

> "For this reason I will confess to You among the Gentiles,
> And sing to Your name."

> And again he says:

> "Rejoice, O Gentiles, with His people!"

> And again:

> "Praise the LORD, all you Gentiles!
> Laud Him, all you peoples!"

> And again, Isaiah says:

> "There shall be a root of Jesse;
> And He who shall rise to reign over the Gentiles,

In Him the Gentiles shall hope."
—Romans 15:9–12

Paul quotes Psalm 117 and Isaiah 11 as being fulfilled in Christ and the church. God's mercy on Israel, through Christ, resulted in salvation coming to the Gentiles (nations). The gospel came to the Jew first. Many Jews responded and were saved. The Gentiles responded to the gospel, and both were made one in Christ. Worship is no longer connected to earthly Jerusalem, but is done in Spirit and truth (John 4:21–24).

> The Spirit of the Lord God is upon me; because the LORD hath anointed me to preach good tidings unto the meek; he hath sent me to bind up the brokenhearted, to proclaim liberty to the captives, and the opening of the prison to them that are bound; to proclaim the acceptable year of the LORD, and the day of vengeance of our God; to comfort all that mourn; to appoint unto them that mourn in Zion, to give

unto them beauty for ashes, the oil of joy for mourning, the garment of praise for the spirit of heaviness; that they might be called trees of righteousness, the planting of the Lord, that he might be glorified.

—Isaiah 61:1–3, kjv

Behold my servant, whom I uphold; mine elect, in whom my soul delighteth; I have put my spirit upon him: he shall bring forth judgment to the Gentiles. He shall not cry, nor lift up, nor cause his voice to be heard in the street. A bruised reed shall he not break, and the smoking flax shall he not quench: he shall bring forth judgment unto truth. He shall not fail nor be discouraged, till he have set judgment in the earth: and the isles shall wait for his law.

—Isaiah 42:1–4, kjv

The kingdom does not come with observation (Luke 17:20). Many in Israel were looking for an earthly kingdom. They were disappointed, and many rejected Christ because He was not an earthly king. Jesus said His kingdom was not of this world. The kingdom is not meat and drink, but righteousness, peace, and joy in the Holy Ghost (Rom. 14:17). The kingdom is spiritual and heavenly.

Jesus told Nicodemus that he must be born again to see the kingdom (John 3:3). In other words, entrance into the kingdom is not by physical birth or genealogy. Physical descent from Abraham did not qualify one to enter the kingdom. The kingdom is spiritual and can be entered into only by spiritual birth.

The language of the prophets is poetic and figurative. The heavens, earth, seas, trees, and waves are commanded to praise the Lord. These are figurative words used to describe nations and peoples. God uses natural symbols and figures to describe spiritual realities. The old covenant types and symbols are present-day realities for the new covenant believer. Righteousness, peace, and joy of the kingdom are found in Christ and His church.

The kingdom of God is within us (Luke 17:21).

The kingdom is Christ in us. You cannot separate Christ and His kingdom. Ezekiel saw a river flowing from the temple, and out of our bellies flow rivers of living water. The kingdom is like a river; it flows from Zion to the nations. Wherever the river goes, it brings healing (Ezek. 47).

One problem we have in understanding "the kingdom of God" is that we think of a kingdom as being a piece of land with fixed boundaries. We think of a place. But in ancient days a king's *kingdom* extended to wherever he could exercise his power. There were no fixed boundaries. Boundaries were fluid and continually changing. The people, therefore, thought in terms of kingly rule. The *kingdom* was the sphere over which each ruler ruled, regardless of boundaries. It was similar to the Bedouin chieftain who is *king* over his people as they travel around in the deserts, no matter where they are. Wherever he is, and wherever he exercises his power, regardless of location, he is king. Thus if his men surround you in the desert because you chance to be where they are, you are in his *kingdom*; you are under his kingly rule. And next year, or even month, the same spot may be under the kingly rule of a Bedouin chieftain of another tribe, while your king is a hundred miles away having taken his *kingdom* with him. They rule over the people, not the land. The word *basileia*, therefore, means, "kingly rule" rather than "kingdom," and it points to submission to a king.*

God's kingdom is evident when the nations come to Zion and worship. We have not come to earthly Zion but to heavenly Zion. The books of the prophets are filled with references to the nations (heathen) coming to worship. This is not a geographical or political nation, but people groups being saved and coming to worship. This has been happening for the past two millennia, and it is happening today.

> But you have come to Mount Zion and to the city of the living God, the heavenly

---

* Angelfire.com, "The Kingdom of God in the New Testament," http://www.angelfire.com/planet/lifetruth/kingdomnew.html (accessed March 26, 2010).

Jerusalem, to an innumerable company of
angels.

—Hebrews 12:22

We have come to Zion, and we are praying that
others will come now and in generations to come.
The kingdom is not geographical (physical), but it
is evident wherever men submit their hearts to the
rule of the king. And as this is done, heaven will be
released on Earth.

Section 2

Prayers and Decrees to Release Heaven on Earth

Lord, Your scepter of leadership comes from Judah, and when You come and reveal Yourself as the Messiah, the nations will gather to You in obedience (Gen. 49:10, AMP).

Lord, Your kingdom is higher than Agag (the kingdom of the Gentiles), and Your kingdom is exalted above all others (Num. 24:7, AMP).

Lord, You are the Star out of Jacob, and You smote the corners of Moab (symbolic enemies of Christ and His church) and destroyed the children of Seth (Moab's sons of tumult) (Num. 24:17, AMP).

Lord, You have been set upon the holy hill of Zion, and You will rule in the midst of Your enemies (Ps. 2:6; 110:2).

Lord, the nations are Your inheritance, and the uttermost parts of the earth Your possession (Ps. 2:8).

Break the nations with Your rod of iron (Ps. 2:9)

Let the kings and judges of the earth be wise, and serve the Lord with reverent awe and worshipful fear, and rejoice with trembling (Ps. 2:10–11).

I will lay me down and sleep, for You, Lord, have sustained me (Ps. 3:5).

Lord, Your blessing is upon my life (Ps. 3:8).

Let the nations offer the sacrifices of righteousness and put their trust in the Lord (Ps. 4:5).

I will lie down and sleep in peace, for You alone, O Lord, make me dwell in safety (Ps. 4:8).

Give heed to the voice of my cry, my King and my God, for to You I will pray (Ps. 5:2).

My voice You shall hear in the morning, O Lord; in the morning I will direct it to You, and I will look up (Ps. 5:3).

Because of your great mercy, I come to Your house, Lord, and I am filled with wonder as I bow down to worship at Your holy temple (Ps. 5:7, CEV).

Lead me, O Lord, in Your righteousness because of my enemies; make Your way straight before my face (Ps. 5:8).

Lord, You have blessed me, and You surround my life with favor (Ps. 5:12).

The Lord has heard my supplication; the Lord will receive my prayer (Ps. 6:9).

My defense is of God, who saves the upright in heart (Ps. 7:10).

Lord, You let us rule everything Your hands have made. And You put all of it under our power—the sheep and the cattle, and every wild animal, the birds in the sky, the fish in the sea, and all ocean creatures. Our Lord and Ruler, Your name is wonderful everywhere on earth! (Ps. 8:6–9, CEV).

Lord, You shall endure forever, and You have prepared Your throne for judgment (Ps. 9:7).

I dwell in Zion, and I will sing praises unto the Lord and declare Your doings among the people (Ps. 9:11).

Once you've pulled me back from the gates of death, I'll write the book on Hallelujahs; on the corner of Main and First I'll hold a street meeting; I'll be the song leader; we'll fill the air with salvation songs (Ps. 9:13–14, The Message).

Put them in fear, O Lord, that the nations may know themselves to be but men (Ps. 9:20).

Arise, O Lord! O God, lift up Your hand! Do not forget the humble (Ps. 10:12).

Our Lord, You will always rule, but nations will vanish from the earth (Ps. 10:16, cev).

You have been good to me, Lord, and I will sing about You (Ps. 13:6, cev).

Lord, Your salvation has come out of Zion, and You have brought back the captivity of Your people; I will rejoice and be glad (Ps. 14:7).

I abide in Your tabernacle, and I dwell in Your holy hill, and I will never be moved (Ps. 15:1, 5).

You, Lord, are all I want! You are my choice, and You keep me safe. You make my life pleasant, and my future is bright (Ps. 16:5–6, cev).

You have made known to me the path of life; You will fill me with joy in Your presence, with eternal pleasures at Your right hand (Ps. 16:11, NIV).

Lord, may my steps always hold closely to Your paths [to the tracks of the One Who has gone on before]; then my feet will not slip from Your paths (Ps. 17:5, AMP).

Keep and guard me as the pupil of Your eye; hide me in the shadow of Your wings (Ps. 17:8, AMP).

Lord, You have promised to light my lamp and to enlighten my darkness (Ps. 18:28).

Lord, because of Your power in me, I can advance against my enemies and scale the walls intended to keep me out (Ps. 18:29, NIV).

Lord, it is You who arms me with strength and makes my way perfect (Ps. 18:32, NIV).

Lord, You give me your shield of victory, and Your right hand sustains me; You stoop down to make me great (Ps. 18:35).

Lord, You enlarge the path under me, so that my feet will not slip (Ps. 18:36).

Let strangers submit to You when they hear of You (Ps. 18:44).

Lord, the heavens declare Your glory, and the skies proclaim the work of Your hands. Your voice has gone out into all the earth, and Your words to the ends of the world (Ps. 19:1, NIV; Rom. 10:18, NIV).

Save, Lord. You are the King; hear me when I call (Ps. 20:9).

Show your strength, Lord, so that we may sing and praise Your power (Ps. 21:13, CEV).

Lord, You inhabit my praise; You are holy (Ps. 22:3).

Lord, everyone on this earth will remember You. People all over the world will turn and worship You, because You are in control, the ruler of all nations (Ps. 22:27–28, CEV).

Surely goodness and mercy shall follow me all the days of my life, and I will dwell in the house of the Lord forever (Ps. 23:6).

Lord, the everlasting gates have opened for You, and You are the King of glory (Ps. 24:7–10).

Show me Your ways, O Lord; teach me Your paths. Lead me in Your truth and teach me, for You are the God of my salvation; on You I wait all the day (Ps. 25:4–5).

Lord, You guide the humble in justice, and You teach the humble Your way (Ps. 25:9).

Lord, because I fear You, You will reveal Your secret to me and will show me Your covenant (Ps. 25:14).

Lord, You are my light and my salvation; whom shall I fear? You are the strength of my life; of whom shall I be afraid? (Ps. 27:1).

One thing I have desired of the Lord, that will I seek: That I may dwell in the house of the Lord all the days of my life, to behold the beauty of the Lord and to inquire in His temple (Ps. 27:4).

Lord, You are my strength and my shield; my heart trusts in You, and I am helped; therefore my heart greatly rejoices, and with my song I will praise You (Ps. 28:7).

Lord, Your voice is powerful, and Your voice is full of majesty (Ps. 29:4).

Lord, the thunder of Your voice can break the cedars into pieces (Ps. 29:5).

Your voice splits and flashes forth forked lightning (Ps. 29:7, AMP).

Lord, Your voice makes the wilderness tremble (Ps. 29:8, AMP).

The voice of the Lord makes deer give birth before their time (Ps. 29:9, CEV).

You have turned for me my mourning into dancing; You have put off my sackcloth and clothed me with gladness (Ps. 30:11).

Blessed be the Lord, for He has shown me His marvelous kindness in a strong city [Zion]! (Ps. 31:21).

My transgression is forgiven, and my sin is covered. I am blessed, my sin is not imputed to me, and there is no guile in my life (Ps. 32:1–2).

Lord, surround me with songs of deliverance (Ps. 32:7).

Let all the earth fear the Lord; let all the inhabitants of the world stand in awe of Him (Ps. 33:8).

Blessed is the nation whose God is the Lord, and the people He has chosen as His own inheritance. I am blessed, and I am a part of the holy nation [the church] (Ps. 33:12; 1 Pet. 2:9).

I put my trust under the shadow of Your wings. I will be abundantly satisfied with the fullness of Your house, and You will give me drink from the river of Your pleasures. With You is the fountain of life, and in Your light I will see light (Ps. 36:7–9).

I delight myself in the Lord, and He gives me the desires of my heart (Ps. 37:4).

I inherit the land, and I delight myself in the abundance of peace [*shalom*] (Ps. 37:11).

Let me not be ashamed in the evil time, and let me be satisfied in the days of famine (Ps. 37:19).

I will wait on You, Lord, and keep Your way; let me be exalted to inherit the land (Ps. 37:34).

Lord, put a new song in my mouth, even praise to You, that many will see it and fear and will trust in the Lord (Ps. 40:3).

I will go with Your people to the house of God with the voice of joy and praise; I will join with them that keep Your festival (Ps. 42:4).

O send out Your light and Your truth. Let them bring me to Your holy hill and to Your dwelling places (Ps. 43:3).

I will worship at Your altar because You make me joyful. You are my God, and I will praise You. Yes, I will praise You as I play my harp (Ps. 43:4, CEV).

Your throne, O God, is forever and ever; a scepter of righteousness is the scepter of Your kingdom. Let the scepter of Your kingdom be stretched over the nations (Ps. 45:6).

There is a river whose streams make glad the city of God, the holy place where the Most High dwells (Ps. 46:4, NIV).

Let the nations be still and know that You are God; be exalted among the nations, and be exalted in the earth (Ps. 46:10).

For the Lord Most High is awesome; He is the great King over all the earth. He will subdue the peoples under us, and the nations under our feet (Ps. 47:2–3).

Let me receive the inheritance You have chosen for me, the glory and pride of Jacob, whom You loved (Ps. 47:4, AMP).

I will sing praises to You, O Lord, my king. You are king over all the earth (Ps. 47:7).

Lord, You reign over the nations; You sit upon the throne of Your holiness (Ps. 47:8).

Let the nobles of the nations assemble as the people of the God of Abraham, for the kings of the earth belong to You (Ps. 47:9).

Lord, You are greatly to be praised in Zion [the church], the city of God, the mountain of Your holiness (Ps. 48:1).

Let Zion be established forever (Ps. 48:8).

Let Mount Zion rejoice, let the daughters of Judah be glad, because of Your judgments (Ps. 48:11).

Lord, let the people, all the inhabitants of the world, give ear and hear Your wisdom. Let them hear and understand Your parables of the kingdom (Ps. 49:1–4).

Lord, speak, and call the earth from the rising of the sun to its going down; out of Zion, let the perfection of Your beauty shine forth (Ps. 50:1–2).

O Lord, open my lips, and my mouth shall show forth Your praise (Ps. 51:15).

Make Zion [the church] the place you delight in; repair Jerusalem's broken-down walls (Ps. 51:18, THE MESSAGE).

But I am like a green olive tree in the house of God; I will trust in the mercy of God forever and ever (Ps. 52:8).

O Lord, Your salvation has come out of Zion, and You have brought back the captivity of Your people; I will rejoice and be glad (Ps. 53:6).

I will freely sacrifice to You; I will praise Your name, O Lord, for it is good (Ps. 54:6).

I cast my burden upon You, Lord, and You will sustain me; You will never permit me to be moved (Ps. 55:22).

In God, whose word I praise, in the Lord, whose word I praise—in God I trust; I will not be afraid. What can man do to me? (Ps. 56:10–11, NIV).

I will praise You, O Lord, among the peoples; I will sing to You among the nations. For Your mercy reaches unto the heavens, and Your truth unto the clouds (Ps. 57:9–10).

Be exalted, O God, above the heavens; let Your glory be above all the earth (Ps. 57:11).

I will sing of Your power, and I will sing aloud of Your mercy, for You have been my defense and refuge in the day of trouble (Ps. 59:16).

Lord, give me Your banner, and let it be displayed because of truth (Ps. 60:4).

Through God I will do valiantly, for it is He who shall tread down our enemies (Ps. 60:12).

I will abide in Your tabernacle forever; I will trust in the shelter of Your wings (Ps. 61:4).

Lord, release Your power, for power belongs to You (Ps. 62:11).

Lord, I have seen you in the sanctuary; let me behold Your power and Your glory (Ps. 63:2).

Lord, my soul will be satisfied as with the richest of foods; with singing lips my mouth will praise You (Ps. 63:5).

Hide me from the secret plots of the wicked, from the rebellion of the workers of iniquity (Ps. 64:2).

Let all flesh come unto You, because You hear prayer (Ps. 65:2).

Bring Your chosen ones near to live in Your courts! Let them be filled with the good things of Your house (Ps. 65:4, NIV).

Answer me with awesome deeds of righteousness (Ps. 65:5).

Still the roaring of the seas, the roaring of their waves, and the turmoil of the nations (Ps. 65:7).

Care for the land and water it; enrich it abundantly from the streams of God that are filled with water to provide the people with grain. Drench its furrows and level its ridges; soften it with showers and bless its crops (Ps. 65:9–10, NIV).

Crown the year with Your bounty, and let Your paths drip with abundance; drop on the pastures of the wilderness, and the little hills will rejoice on every side (Ps. 65:11–12).

Let the pastures be clothed with flocks, and the valleys also be covered with grain; let them shout for joy and sing (Ps. 65:13).

Make a joyful shout to God, all the earth (Ps. 66:1).

Sing out the honor of His name; make His praise glorious (Ps. 66:2).

How awesome are Your works! Through the greatness of Your power Your enemies shall submit themselves to You (Ps. 66:3).

Let all the earth worship You and sing unto You; they will sing praises to Your name (Ps. 66:4).

Lord, rule by Your power forever, and let Your eyes observe the nations; do not let the rebellious exalt themselves (Ps. 66:7).

Lord, bring me into a place of abundance (Ps. 66:12).

Let God arise, let His enemies be scattered; let those also who hate Him flee before Him (Ps. 68:1).

I will be glad and rejoice before my God, and I will exceedingly rejoice (Ps. 68:3).

Let the nations sing unto God, "Our God, You are the one who rides on the clouds, and we praise You. Your name is the Lord, and we celebrate as we worship You" (Ps. 68:4, CEV).

Lord, set the lonely in families, and lead forth the prisoners with singing; but let the rebellious live in a sun-scorched land (Ps. 68:6, NIV).

The earth trembled, the heavens also poured down [rain] at the presence of God. You, O God, did send a plentiful rain; You did restore and confirm Your heritage when it languished and was weary (Ps. 68:8–9, AMP).

Lord, give the word, and let a great company publish it (Ps. 68:11).

Sing to God, you kingdoms of the earth; oh, sing praises to the Lord (Ps. 68:32).

You have saved Zion and built the cities of Judah [praise]. I will dwell in Zion and have it in possession (Ps. 69:35).

I inherit Zion; I dwell in Zion because I love Your name (Ps. 69:36).

In You, O Lord, I put my trust; let me never be put to shame (Ps. 71:1).

I have become as a wonder to many, but You are my strong refuge (Ps. 71:7).

I will go in the strength of the Lord God; I will make mention of Your righteousness, of Yours only (Ps. 71:16).

Lord, increase my greatness, and comfort me on every side (Ps. 71:21).

Let the mountains bring peace [shalom] to the people, and the hills, through [the general establishment of] righteousness (Ps. 72:3, AMP).

Lord, bring justice to the poor of the people; save the children of the needy, and break in pieces the oppressor (Ps. 72:4).

Let the nations fear You as long as the sun and moon endure, throughout all generations (Ps. 72:5).

Lord, come down as rain upon the mown grass, as showers that water the earth (Ps. 72:6).

Lord, I live in the days of the kingdom; let the righteous flourish and have abundance of peace [*shalom*], until the moon is no more (Ps. 72:7).

Let Your dominion be from sea to sea, and from the River to the ends of the earth (Ps. 72:8).

Let those in the wilderness bow before You, Lord, and let Your enemies lick the dust (Ps. 72:9).

Let the kings of Tarshish and Sheba offer gifts (Ps. 72:10).

Let all kings bow down, and let all nations serve You (Ps. 72:11).

Lord, deliver the needy when they cry, and the poor who have no helper. Spare the poor and needy, and spare the souls of the needy (Ps. 72:12–13).

Your name will endure forever, and Your name shall continue as long as the sun. Men will be blessed in You, and all nations will call You blessed (Ps. 72:17).

Blessed be Your glorious name forever! Let the whole earth be filled with Your glory (Ps. 72:19).

Crush the heads of Leviathan, and give him as food for the creatures inhabiting the wilderness (Ps. 74:14, AMP).

Cut off the horns of the wicked, and let the horns of the righteous be exalted (Ps. 75:10).

Cut off the spirit [of pride and fury] of princes; You are terrible to the [ungodly] kings of the earth (Ps. 76:12).

Let the groaning of the prisoner come before You; according to the greatness of Your power preserve those who are appointed to die (Ps. 79:11).

The haters of the Lord will pretend submission to You, but their fate will endure forever (Ps. 81:15).

Let men know that You, whose name is Jehovah, are the Most High over all the earth (Ps. 83:18).

I will go from strength to strength and appear before You, Lord, in Zion (Ps. 84:7).

Lord, You are a sun and shield; You give grace and glory; no good thing will You withhold from those who walk uprightly (Ps. 84:11).

Lord, You have been favorable to me and brought back my captivity; You have forgiven my iniquity and covered all my sin (Ps. 85:1–2).

Let truth spring out of the earth, and let righteousness look down from heaven (Ps. 85:11).

Let all nations come and worship before You, O Lord, and let them glorify Your name (Ps. 86:9).

Show that You approve of me! Then my hateful enemies will feel like fools, because You have helped and comforted me (Ps. 86:17, CEV).

Lord, You love the gates of Zion [the church], and glorious things are spoken of Zion, the city of God (Ps. 87:2–3).

Lord, I am born in Zion; let Zion be established in all the earth (Ps. 87:5).

You will satisfy me with long life and show me Your salvation (Ps. 91:16).

My horn (emblem of excessive strength and stately grace) You have exalted like that of a wild ox; I am anointed with fresh oil (Ps. 92:10, AMP).

I will flourish like the palm tree and grow like a cedar in Lebanon (Ps. 92:12).

I am planted in the house of the Lord and flourish in the courts of my God (Ps. 92:13).

I am [growing in grace] and will still bring forth fruit in old age; I will be full of sap [of spiritual vitality] and [rich in the] verdure [of trust, love, and contentment] (Ps. 92:14, AMP).

The Lord reigns, He is clothed with majesty; the Lord is robed, He has girded Himself with strength and power; the world also is established, that it cannot be moved (Ps. 93:1, AMP).

Lord, subdue the floods that have lifted up, for You are mightier than the noise of many waters (Ps. 93:3–4).

I will sing unto the Lord a new song. Let the earth sing unto the Lord (Ps. 96:1).

I will proclaim the good news of Your salvation from day to day (Ps. 96:2).

I will declare Your glory among the nations, and Your wonders among all people (Ps. 96:3).

Let the families of the peoples give to the Lord glory and strength. Let them give to the Lord the glory due His name; let them bring an offering and come into His courts (Ps. 96:7–8).

Let the nations worship the Lord in the beauty of holiness, and fear before Him (Ps. 96:9).

Let the earth be firmly established, and let the nations say, "The Lord reigns" (Ps. 96:10).

Let the heavens rejoice, let the earth be glad; let the sea resound, and all that is in it (Ps. 96:11, NIV).

Let the fields be jubilant, and everything in them. Then all the trees of the forest will sing for joy (Ps. 96:12).

Lord, You reign. Let the earth rejoice; let the multitude of the islands be glad (Ps. 97:1).

Let the heavens declare Your righteousness, and all the people see Your glory (Ps. 97:6).

I will sing unto You a new song, for You have done marvelous things (Ps. 98:1).

Lord, make Your salvation known, and reveal Your righteousness to the nations (Ps. 98:2).

Shout for joy to the Lord, all the earth; burst into jubilant song with music (Ps. 98:4).

Let the sea resound, and everything in it; the world, and all who live in it (Ps. 98:7).

Let the rivers clap their hands, let the mountains sing together for joy; let them sing before the Lord (Ps. 98:8–9, NIV).

Lord, You reign; let the people tremble, for You are great in Zion (Ps. 99:1–2).

Lord, Your word says that it is the set, appointed time to favor Zion. As a citizen of Zion, I declare that I walk in the favor of God. It is the appointed time for Your favor to abound and increase toward me (Ps. 102:13).

Lord, build up Zion and appear in Your glory, so the nations can fear You, and all the kings of the earth see Your glory (Ps. 102:15–16).

Lord, You will hear the prayer of the destitute, and You will not despise their prayer (Ps. 102:17).

Lord, You will look down from the height of Your sanctuary and will hear the groaning of the prisoner and will release those appointed to death (Ps. 102:19–20).

I will praise the Lord from my inmost being, and I will forget not all His benefits (Ps. 103:2).

Lord, You forgive all my sins and heal all my diseases (Ps. 103:3, NIV).

Lord, You have redeemed my life from the pit, and You have crowned me with love and compassion (Ps. 103:4, NIV).

You satisfy my desires with good things, so that my youth is renewed like the eagle's (Ps. 103:5).

Lord, work righteousness and justice for all the oppressed (Ps. 103:6, NIV).

As far as the east is from the west, so far have You removed my transgression from me (Ps. 103:12).

Lord, You have established Your throne in heaven, and Your kingdom rules over all (Ps. 103:19).

All of God's creation and all that He rules, come and praise the Lord! With all my heart I praise the Lord! (Ps. 103:22).

How many are your works, O Lord! In wisdom You made them all; the earth is full of Your creatures (Ps. 104:24, NIV).

May the glory of the Lord endure forever; may the Lord rejoice in his works (Ps. 104:31, NIV).

Lord, turn my desert into pools of water and my parched ground into flowing springs (Ps. 107:35, NIV).

Lord, send forth from Zion the scepter of Your strength; rule, then, in the midst of Your foes (Ps. 110:2, AMP).

Lord, give me meat, and be ever mindful of Your covenant (Ps. 111:5).

Lord, You sent redemption to Your people, and You have commanded Your covenant forever; holy and reverent is Your name (Ps. 111:9).

From the rising of the sun to its going down, the Lord's name is to be praised. The Lord is high above all nations, His glory above the heavens (Ps. 113:3–4).

Raise the poor out of the dust, and lift the needy out of the ash heap (Ps. 113:7).

Grant the barren woman a home, like a joyful mother of children (Ps. 113:9).

Tremble, O earth, at the presence of the Lord, at the presence of the God of Jacob (Ps. 114:7).

All of you nations, come praise the Lord! Let everyone praise Him. His love for us is wonderful; His faithfulness never ends. Shout praises to the Lord! (Ps. 117).

Shouts of joy and victory resound in the tents of the righteous: "The Lord's right hand has done mighty things!" (Ps. 118:15).

Lord, You have opened the gates of righteousness; I will go into them, and I will praise You (Ps. 118:19).

The stone which the builders rejected has become the chief cornerstone. This was the Lord's doing; it is marvelous in my eyes (Ps. 118:22–23).

This is the day You have made; I will rejoice and be glad in it (Ps. 118:24).

Save now, we beseech You, O Lord; send now prosperity, O Lord, we beseech You, and give to us success! (Ps. 118:25, AMP).

The Lord is your keeper; the Lord is your shade at your right hand. The sun shall not strike you by day, nor the moon by night. The Lord shall preserve you from all evil; He shall preserve your soul (Ps. 121:5–7).

The Lord will preserve my going out and my coming in from this time forth, and even forevermore (Ps. 121:8).

Let peace [*shalom*] be within my walls, and prosperity within my palace (Ps. 122:7).

Lord, surround Your people as the mountains surround Jerusalem, from this time forth and forever (Ps. 125:2).

Let Your priests be clothed with righteousness, and let Your saints shout for joy (Ps. 132:9).

Lord, You have chosen Zion [Your church] and have desired it for Your dwelling place. This is

Your resting place forever; here You dwell, for You have desired it (Ps. 132:13–14).

Bless my provision, and satisfy me with bread (Ps. 132:15).

Clothe me with salvation, and I will shout aloud for joy (Ps. 132:16).

Lord, command Your blessing upon Zion [the church], even life forevermore (Ps. 133:3).

I will lift up my hands in the sanctuary, and I will bless the Lord. Lord, You made heaven and earth, and you will bless me out of Zion (Ps. 134:2–3).

Lord, Your mercy endures forever (Ps. 136).

Let all the kings of the earth praise You when they hear the words of Your mouth (Ps. 138:4).

Lord, perfect that which concerns me, for Your mercy endures forever (Ps. 138:8).

I will praise You, O Lord, for I am fearfully and wonderfully made (Ps. 139:14).

Lord, Your thoughts are precious unto me; how great is the sum of them! They are more in number than the sand (Ps. 139:17–18).

Set a guard, O Lord, over my mouth; keep watch over the door of my lips (Ps. 141:3).

I pray to you, Lord! You are my place of safety, and You are my choice in the land of the living. Please answer my prayer. I am completely helpless. Help! They are chasing me, and they are too strong. Rescue me from this prison, so I can praise Your name. And when Your people notice Your wonderful kindness to me, they will rush to my side (Ps. 142:5–7, CEV).

Cause me to hear Your lovingkindness in the morning, for in You do I trust; cause me to know the way in which I should walk, for I lift up my soul to You (Ps. 143:8).

Teach me to do Your will, for You are my God; Your Spirit is good. Lead me in the land of uprightness (Ps. 143:10).

Lord, You are my steadfast love and my fortress, my high tower and my deliverer, my shield and He in whom I trust and take refuge, who subdues my people under me (Ps. 144:2).

Let our sons be as plants grown up in their youth (Ps. 144:12).

Let our daughters be as pillars, sculptured in palace style (Ps. 144:12).

Let our barns be full, supplying all kinds of produce (Ps. 144:13).

Let our sheep bring forth thousands and ten thousands in our fields (Ps. 144:13).

Let our oxen be strong to labor; that there be no breaking in or going out; that there be no complaining in our streets. Happy am I, whose God is the Lord (Ps. 144:14–15).

Let this generation praise Your works to the next, and declare Your mighty acts (Ps. 145:4).

I will meditate on the glorious splendor of Your majesty, and on Your wondrous works (Ps. 145:5).

Men shall speak of the might of Your awesome acts, and I will declare Your greatness (Ps. 145:6).

Let men speak of the glory of Your kingdom and talk of Your power (Ps. 145:11).

Your kingdom is an everlasting kingdom, and Your dominion endures throughout all generations (Ps. 145:13).

Lord, give freedom to the prisoners (Ps. 146:7).

Lord, open the eyes of the blind, and raise up those who are bowed down (Ps. 146:8).

Lord, watch over the strangers and relieve the fatherless and widow, but turn the way of the wicked upside down (Ps. 146:9).

Let Your kingdom and reign touch this generation (Ps. 146:10).

Lord, build up Jerusalem [Your church], and gather together the outcasts of Israel (Ps. 147:2).

Lord, heal the brokenhearted, and bind up their wounds (Ps. 147:3).

Lord, lift up the humble, but cast the wicked to the ground (Ps. 147:6).

Lord, make peace within my borders, and fill me with the finest of wheat (Ps. 147:14).

Let the heavens, the heights, the angels, the sun, the moon, and stars of light praise You, Lord. Let the heavens of heavens, the waters above the heavens, praise the name of the Lord: for He commanded, and they were created (Ps. 148:1–5).

Praise the Lord from the earth, you great sea creatures and all the depths; fire and hail, snow and clouds; stormy wind, fulfilling His word; mountains and all hills; fruitful trees and all cedars; beasts and all cattle; creeping things and flying fowl; kings of the earth and all peoples; princes and all judges of the earth; both young men and maidens; old men and children. Let them praise the name of the Lord, for His name alone is exalted; His glory is above the earth and heaven (Ps. 148:7–13).

Praise the Lord! Sing to the Lord a new song, and His praise in the assembly of saints (Ps. 149:1).

I will rejoice in Him who made me. Let Zion be joyful in their King (Ps. 149:2).

Lord, take pleasure in me, and beautify me with salvation (Ps. 149:4).

Where the word of a king is, there is power; Lord, release Your word (Eccles. 8:4).

Let the nations come to the mountain of the house of the Lord [the church], and let them learn His ways and walk in His paths. Let them beat their swords into plowshares, and their spears into pruninghooks, and let them learn war no more (Isa. 2:2–4).

Let the people who walk in darkness and in the shadow of death see Your light (Isa. 9:2).

Of the increase of Your government and peace [*shalom*], there is no end. Let Your government and peace increase from generation to generation (Isa. 9:7).

Let Your remnant, Your elect, depend on You, the Holy One of Israel. Let Your remnant return to You as the sand of the sea, for the destruction decreed shall overflow with righteousness (Isa. 10:20–22).

Lord, You are the root of Jesse, and You stand as a banner to Your people. Let the nations seek You and enter into Your glorious rest (Isa. 11:10).

God is my salvation. I will trust and not be afraid, for the Lord Jehovah is my strength and my song; He has become my salvation (Isa. 12:2).

With joy will I draw water from the wells of salvation (Isa. 12:3).

I will praise the Lord, call upon His name, declare His doings among the people, and make mention that His name is exalted (Isa. 12:4).

I will sing unto the Lord, for He has done excellent things; this is known in all the earth (Isa. 12:5).

I will cry out and shout, because I am an inhabitant of Zion, and great is the Holy One of Israel in my midst (Isa. 12:6).

Let me enjoy the rest I have in Christ. I have rest from sorrow and from fear and from hard bondage (Isa. 14:3).

The whole earth [the church] is at rest and is quiet; let them [the church] break forth into singing (Isa. 14:7).

Let the trees [the church] rejoice at the fall of the oppressor (Isa. 14:8).

Lord, exactly as You planned, it will happen. These are Your blueprints, it will take shape. You will shatter the enemies who trespass on Your land and will stomp them into the dirt on Your mountains. You will ban them from taking and making slaves of Your people and will lift the weight of oppression from all shoulders. This is Your plan, planned for the whole earth. And it is Your hand that will do it, reaching into every nation. God-of-the-Angel-Armies has planned it. Who could ever cancel such plans? Your hand has reached out. Who could brush it aside? (Isa. 14:24–27, The Message).

Lord, Your throne is established in mercy, and You sit upon it in truth in the tabernacle of David, judging and seeking justice and hastening righteousness (Isa. 16:5).

Lord, on Mount [Zion] You will make for all peoples a feast of rich things [symbolic of Your coronation festival inaugurating the reign of the Lord on earth, in the wake of a background of gloom, judgment, and terror], a feast of wines on the lees—of fat things full of marrow, of wines on the lees well refined. And You will destroy on this mountain the covering of the face that is cast over the heads of all peoples [in mourning], and the veil [of profound wretchedness] that is woven and spread over all nations (Isa. 25:6–7, AMP).

Lord, I sing a new song. I have a strong city; salvation is appointed for walls and bulwarks (Isa. 26:1).

The gates of Zion are opened; let the righteous nation that keeps Your truth enter (Isa. 26:2).

You will keep me in perfect peace, because my mind is stayed on You, and I trust in You (Isa. 26:3).

I will trust in the Lord forever; for in the Lord Jehovah is everlasting strength (Isa. 26:4).

Lord, You will establish peace [*shalom*] for us (Isa. 26:12).

You will [deliver Israel from her enemies and also from the rebel powers of evil and darkness]. Your sharp and unrelenting, great, and strong sword will visit and punish Leviathan the swiftly fleeing serpent, Leviathan the twisting and winding serpent (Isa. 27:1, AMP).

I will sing the song of Your church, a fruitful vineyard. You will water me every moment, and guard me night and day so that no one may harm me (Isa. 27:2–3).

Lord, You have laid a stone in Zion [Your church] and placed it for a foundation, a stone, a tried stone, a precious cornerstone, a sure foundation, and I will never be dismayed because I trust You (Isa. 28:16).

Lord, You long to be gracious to me; You rise to show me compassion. You are a God of justice. I will wait for You and be blessed (Isa. 30:18, NIV).

I hear the voice of the Lord. He tells me the way, when I should turn to the right, or to the left, and counsels me to walk in the way (Isa. 30:21).

I have a song, and gladness of heart, and I come to the mountain of the Lord, to the Mighty One of Israel (Isa. 30:29).

Let Your Spirit be poured out from on high, and the wilderness be a fruitful field, and the fruitful field be counted for a forest (Isa. 32:15).

Let righteousness work peace in my life, and let the effect of righteousness be quietness and confidence forever (Isa. 32:17, NIV).

Let me dwell in a peaceful dwelling place, and in secure homes, in undisturbed places of rest (Isa. 32:18, NIV).

Lord, be gracious to me; I long for you. Be my strength every morning, my salvation in time of distress (Isa. 33:2, NIV).

Let wisdom and knowledge be my stability, and strength of salvation, and the fear of the Lord my treasure (Isa. 33:6).

Lord, I will walk righteously and speak uprightly; I will despise gain from fraud and from oppression, and will shake my hand free from the taking of bribes; I will stop my ears from hearing of bloodshed and shut my eyes to avoid looking upon evil. Therefore You will cause me to dwell on the heights; my place of defense will be the fortresses of rocks; bread will be given to me, and water for me will be sure (Isa. 33:15–16, NIV).

Let my eyes see Your beauty, Lord (Isa. 33:17).

Let Your church be as secure as a tent with pegs that cannot be pulled up and fastened with ropes that can never be broken (Isa. 33:20, CEV).

Lord, be unto me a place of broad rivers and streams (Isa. 33:21).

I will not say I am sick, because my iniquity is forgiven (Isa. 33:24).

Let every wilderness and solitary place in my life rejoice, and blossom abundantly as a rose (Isa. 35:1).

Let rejoicing, joy, and singing come into every wilderness place (Isa. 35:2).

Let the glory of Lebanon, the excellence of Carmel and Sharon, come into my life, and let me see the glory of the Lord (Isa. 35:2).

Strengthen my weak hands, and make firm my feeble knees (Isa. 35:3).

Let my eyes be opened, and every blind area of my life be removed (Isa. 35:5).

Let my ears be opened, and let every deaf area of life be unstopped (Isa. 35:5).

Let every lame area of my life be healed, and let me leap like a deer (Isa. 35:6).

Let my tongue sing for joy, and let waters and streams break out in every area of my life (Isa. 35:6).

Let every parched area of my life become a pool, and every thirsty area of my life a spring of water (Isa. 35:7).

Let me walk on the highway of holiness, and let no lion or ravenous beast be in my path, for I am the redeemed of the Lord (Isa. 35:8–9).

I will come to Zion with songs and everlasting joy upon my head (Isa. 35:10).

I will obtain joy and gladness, and sorrow and sighing will flee from my life (Isa. 35:10).

I receive the comfort of the Lord, my iniquity is pardoned, and my warfare is accomplished (Isa. 40:1–2).

The way of the LORD is made straight in my life, and a highway has been made in my life for my God (Isa. 40:3).

Let every valley in my life be exalted, and every mountain be made low (Isa. 40:4).

Lord, make the crooked places in my life straight, and every rough place smooth (Isa. 40:4).

Let the glory of the Lord be revealed in my life, for You, Lord, have spoken it (Isa. 40:5).

I will go to the mountain of the Lord, and I will lift up my voice with strength and declare, "Behold your God!" (Isa. 40:9).

Lord, I am a part of Your flock; feed me, and gently lead me (Isa. 40:11).

Lord, give me power and increase my strength. (Isa. 40:29).

I will wait upon the Lord and renew my strength. (Isa. 40:31).

I will mount up with wings as an eagle; I will run and not be weary, I will walk and not be faint. (Isa. 40:31).

___

Lord, I will not fear, for You are with me; You strengthen me, help me, and uphold me with Your righteous right hand (Isa. 41:10).

___

I will not fear, for You, Lord, will hold my hand and help me (Isa. 41:13).

___

Lord, You have allowed me to become like a log covered with sharp spikes. You will help me to grind and crush every mountain and hill until they turn to dust. A strong wind will scatter them in all directions (Isa. 41:15–16, CEV).

___

Lord, open rivers in high places for me, and fountains in the midst of my valley (Isa. 41:18).

___

Lord, in every desert place in my life, You will fill the desert with all kinds of trees—cedars, acacias, and myrtles; olive and cypress trees; fir trees and pines (Isa. 41:19).

___

Everyone will see and know, and consider and understand together, that the hand of the Lord has done this in my life, and that I am Your new creation (Isa. 41:20).

Lord, establish Your justice in the earth, and let the coastlands receive Your law (Isa. 42:4).

Let the blind eyes be opened, bring out the prisoners from prison, and those that sit in darkness out of the prison house (Isa. 42:7).

Let new things be declared in my life, and let them spring forth (Isa. 42:9).

I will sing unto You a new song and release Your praise from my life (Isa. 42:10).

Let the wilderness areas in my life lift up their voices, and let me shout from the top of the mountains (Isa. 42:11).

I will give You glory and declare Your praise (Isa. 42:12).

Lord, go forth as a mighty man; cry, roar, and prevail against Your enemies (Isa. 42:13).

Lord, bring the blind by a way they know not, and lead them in paths they have not known. (Isa. 42:16).

Make darkness light before me, and crooked things straight in my life (Isa. 42:16).

Lord, magnify Your law, and make it honorable (Isa. 42:21).

Lord, You have redeemed me; You have summoned me by name; I am Yours. I will not be afraid (Isa. 43:1, NIV).

When I pass through the waters, You will be with me; the rivers will not overflow my life (Isa. 43:2).

When I walk through the fire, I will not be burned, and the flames will not set me ablaze (Isa. 43:2).

Lord, You have brought me from the ends of the earth and joined me to the Holy One of Israel (Isa. 43:3–6).

Lord, You have created me for Your glory; You have formed me and made me (Isa. 43:7).

Lord, I am Your witness, I am Your servant, You have chosen me, and there is no other God beside You (Isa. 43:10–11).

Lord, make a way in the sea and a path in the mighty waters (Isa. 43:16).

Lord, You drew out the chariots and horses, the army and reinforcements together, and they lay there, never to rise again, extinguished, snuffed out like a wick (Isa. 43:17, NIV).

Lord, help me to forget the former things and not to dwell on the past. Do a new thing in my life. Make a way in the wilderness and rivers in the desert (Isa. 43:19).

Let the wild animals of the field honor You, the jackals and the owls, because You provide water in the wilderness and streams in the wasteland to give drink to me, Your chosen (Isa. 43:20).

Lord, You have formed me for Yourself, and I will show forth Your praise (Isa. 43:21).

Lord, You have blotted out my sins for Your sake, and You will not remember my sins (Isa. 43:25).

Pour water upon every thirsty place of my life and floods upon every dry place in my life (Isa. 44:3).

Pour Your spirit on my descendants and blessing upon my offspring (Isa. 44:3, NIV).

Let my offspring spring up like grass or like willow trees near flowing streams to worship You and to be Your people (Isa. 44:4, NIV).

You have swept away my offenses like a cloud, like the morning mist. I have returned to You, for You have redeemed me (Isa. 44:22, NIV).

Let the heavens sing, and let the lower parts of the earth shout, for the Lord has done this (Isa. 44:23, NIV).

Let the mountains, the forest, and every tree sing, for the Lord has redeemed me (Isa. 44:23, NIV).

Lord, foil the signs of false prophets and make fools of diviners; overthrow the learning of the wise and turn it into nonsense (Isa. 44:25, NIV).

Carry out the words of Your servants, and fulfill the predictions of Your messengers (Isa. 44:26, NIV).

Let Jerusalem, Your church, be inhabited, let the cities of Judah (praise) be built, and let the decayed places be restored (Isa. 44:26, NIV).

Let the deep be dry, and dry up the rivers, that Your anointed may cross over (Isa. 44:27–28, NIV).

Lord, I am Your anointed. Take me by the right hand, and subdue nations, strip kings of their armor, and open doors before me so that gates will not be shut (Isa. 45:1, NIV).

Go before me, and level the mountains, break the gates of brass, and cut through the bars of iron (Isa. 45:2, NIV).

Give me the treasures of darkness and hidden riches of secret places (Isa. 45:3, NIV).

Let the heavens rain down, and the skies pour down righteousness. Let the earth open and bring forth salvation, and let righteousness spring up together (Isa. 45:8).

Let the nations come and fall down, saying, "God is in you, and there is no other god" (Isa. 45:14).

I am saved with an everlasting salvation, and the Lord will always keep me safe and free from shame (Isa. 45:17, CEV).

Let the ends of the earth look unto You and be saved (Isa. 45:22).

In the Lord I have righteousness and strength (Isa. 45:24).

I am justified in the Lord, and I glory in His salvation (Isa. 45:25).

Let every idol bow and stoop before the Lord (Isa. 46:1).

Lord, You declare the end from the beginning. Let Your counsel stand, and do all Your pleasure (Isa. 46:10).

Lord, You have placed Your righteousness and salvation in Zion (Isa. 46:13).

Teach me to profit, and lead me in the way I should go (Isa. 48:17).

Lord, You are a light to the nations, and Your salvation goes to the ends of the earth (Isa. 49:6).

Let kings see You and arise; let princes fall down and worship, because You are faithful and have chosen me (Isa. 49:7).

Lord, You have said that You will answer my prayers and have set a time when You will come to save me. You have chosen me to take Your promise of hope to other nations. You will rebuild the country from its ruins, and then people will come and settle there (Isa. 49:8, cev).

You will set prisoners free from dark dungeons to see the light of day. On their way home, they will find plenty to eat, even on barren hills. They won't go hungry or get thirsty; they won't be bothered by the scorching sun or hot desert winds. You will be merciful while leading them along to streams of water (Isa. 49:9–10, cev).

Let Your mountains become a way, and let Your highways be exalted (Isa. 49:11).

Shout for joy, O heavens; rejoice, O earth; burst into song, O mountains! For the Lord comforts His people and will have compassion on His afflicted ones (Isa. 49:13, NIV).

Let our children make haste, and let the destroyers go forth out of my life (Isa. 49:17).

Lord, thank You for Your promise to signal all the nations to return our sons and our daughters to the arms of Jerusalem [the church] (Isa. 49:22, CEV).

Let kings and queens bow down to You, and let those who wait for You not be ashamed (Isa. 49:23).

Let the captives of the mighty be taken away and the prey of the terrible be delivered (Isa. 49:25).

Lord, You have comforted Zion [the church] and looked with compassion on all her ruins (Isa. 51:3, NIV).

Lord, cause my desert places to be like the Garden of Eden, and my wastelands like the garden of the Lord. Fill me with joy and gladness, thanksgiving, and the sound of singing (Isa. 51:3, NIV).

Lord, was it not You who dried up the sea, the waters of the great deep, who made a road in the depths of the sea so that the redeemed might cross over? (Isa. 51:10, NIV).

You have ransomed me and caused me to enter Zion with singing; You have given me a crown of everlasting joy and gladness, and sorrow and sighing will flee away (Isa. 51:11, NIV).

Lord, You have put Your words in my mouth and covered me with the shadow of Your hand, that You might plant the heavens, lay the foundations of the earth, and say unto Zion, "You are My people" (Isa. 51:16).

I will awake, put on strength, and put on my beautiful garments, and nothing unclean will come through my life (Isa. 52:1).

I shake myself and loose myself from the bands of my neck, for I am redeemed without money (Isa. 52:2–3).

Let the gospel of the kingdom be preached; let the good tidings of peace be published; I will declare, "My God reigns" (Isa. 52:7).

Let the waste places break forth into joy and sing together, for You have comforted Your people (Isa. 52:9).

Make bare Your holy arm in the eyes of all nations, and let the ends of the earth see Your salvation (Isa. 52:10).

Lord, go before me and be my rear guard (Isa. 52:12).

Lord, sprinkle many nations; let them see, and those who have not heard, let them consider (Isa. 52:15).

I have believed Your report, and Your arm is revealed unto me (Isa. 53:1).

Lord, You have borne my griefs and carried my sorrows; You were wounded for my transgressions and bruised for my iniquities; the chastisement for my peace was upon You, and by Your stripes I am healed (Isa. 53:4–5).

I will sing and shout for joy, for You have told me to enlarge the place of my tent and to stretch my tent curtains wide, for my descendants will dispossess nations and settle in their desolate cities (Isa. 54:1–3, NIV).

I will not be afraid and I will not be ashamed, for the LORD is my maker, and He is the God of the whole earth (Isa. 54:5).

Lord, though the mountains be shaken and the hills be removed, Your unfailing love for me will not be shaken and Your covenant of peace will not be removed from my life, for You have had compassion on me (Isa. 54:10, NIV).

Although I have been lashed by storms, You have promised to build me with stones of turquoise and my foundations with sapphires. You will make battlements for me of rubies and gates of sparkling jewels and all my walls of precious stones (Isa. 54:11–12, NIV).

I am taught of the LORD, and I have great peace [*shalom*] (Isa. 54:13).

I am established in righteousness, and tyranny will be far from me; I will have nothing to fear, for terror will be far removed and will not come near me (Isa. 54:14, NIV).

No weapon forged against me will prevail, and I will refute every tongue that accuses me, for this is my heritage and my vindication from the Lord (Isa. 54:17, NIV).

I receive the everlasting covenant, and I receive the sure mercies of David (Isa. 55:3).

I go out with joy, and I am led forth with peace; the mountains and the hills break forth before me into singing, and all the trees of the field clap their hands (Isa. 55:12).

Cypress and myrtle trees will grow in fields once covered by thorns. And then those trees will stand as a lasting witness to the glory of the Lord (Isa. 55:13, CEV).

Lord, You have given me a place within Your walls, and You have given me a name, an everlasting name, that shall not be cut off (Isa. 56:5).

I have come to the mountain of the Lord, and I am joyful in the house of prayer, and I offer to God the sacrifices of praise (Isa. 56:7).

Lord, let my light break forth as the morning, let my health spring forth speedily, let my righteousness go before me, and let You, Lord, be my rear guard (Isa. 58:8).

Lord, guide me continually, and satisfy my soul in drought, and strengthen my bones; let me be like a watered garden and like a spring of water, whose waters fail not (Isa. 58:11).

Lord, let me build up the old waste places, and let me raise up the foundations of many generations; let me be the repairer of the breach and the restorer of paths to dwell in (Isa. 58:12, KJV).

Lord, I delight in You; cause me to ride upon the high places of the earth, and feed me with the heritage of Jacob, for Your mouth has spoken it (Isa. 58:14).

Let the nations fear You from the west, and Your glory from the rising of the sun (Isa. 59:19).

When the enemy comes in like a flood, the Spirit of the Lord shall lift up a standard against him (Isa. 59:19).

Lord, I receive Your covenant, and Your Spirit is upon me, and Your words are in my mouth (Isa. 59:21).

Let Your church arise and shine, for the glory of the Lord is risen upon us (Isa. 60:1).

Let the glory of the Lord be seen upon the church, and let those in darkness come to the light, and see the brightness of our rising (Isa. 60:2–3).

Let the sons and daughters of the nations come to Zion (Isa. 60:4).

Let our hearts swell with joy, because the abundance of the sea shall be turned to us, and the wealth of the Gentiles shall come to Zion [the church] (Isa. 60:5).

Zion's gates are open continually; they are not shut day or night, that men may bring the wealth of the nations (Isa. 60:11).

Let the glory of Lebanon come to Zion, let Your sanctuary be beautified, and let the place of Your feet be glorious (Isa. 60:13).

We are the city of the Lord, the Zion of the Holy One of Israel (Isa. 60:14).

Lord, [instead of the tyranny of the present] You will appoint peace as your officers and righteousness as your taskmasters (Isa. 60:17, AMP).

Violence shall no more be heard in my land, nor devastation or destruction within my borders, but I will call my walls Salvation and my gates Praise (Isa. 60:18, AMP).

The Lord is my everlasting light, and my God is my glory (Isa. 60:19).

Lord, this is what You have promised: "Your sun will never set or your moon go down. I, the

Lord, will be your everlasting light, and your days of sorrow will come to an end. Your people will live right and always own the land; they are the trees I planted to bring praise to me. Even the smallest family will be a powerful nation," for You are the Lord, and when the time comes, You will quickly accomplish Your Word (Isa. 60:20–22, CEV).

Lord, You give me beauty for ashes, the oil of joy for mourning, the garment of praise for the spirit of heaviness; that I may be called a tree of righteousness, Your planting, that You may be glorified (Isa. 61:3).

I am a priest of the Lord, a servant of God, and I eat the riches of the nations (Isa. 61:6).

Instead of shame, I will receive double honor (Isa. 61:7).

I receive the everlasting covenant, and I am the seed that the Lord has blessed (Isa. 61:8–9).

I delight greatly in the Lord; my soul rejoices in my God. For he has clothed me with garments of salvation and arrayed me in a robe of righteousness (Isa. 61:10, NIV).

Let righteousness and praise spring forth before all nations (Isa. 61:11).

Let the nations see Your righteousness, and all kings Your glory (Isa. 62:2).

I am a crown of glory in the hand of the Lord, and a royal diadem in the hand of my God (Isa. 62:3).

I [Judah] will no more be termed Forsaken, nor shall my land be called Desolate any more. I will be called Hephzibah [My delight is in her], and my land be called Beulah [married]; for the Lord delights in me, and my land shall be married [owned and protected by the Lord] (Isa. 62:4, AMP).

I will give You no rest until Jerusalem [the church] is established and made a praise in the earth (Isa. 62:7).

I will eat and drink in the courts of Your holiness (Isa. 62:9, KJV).

I am the redeemed of the Lord, and I am sought out, a city not forsaken (Isa. 62:12).

I will mention the loving-kindnesses of the Lord and the praises of the Lord, according to all that the Lord has bestowed on me, and the great goodness toward the house of Israel [the church], which He has bestowed on them according to His mercies, according to the multitude of His loving-kindnesses (Isa. 63:7).

Since ancient times no one has heard, no ear has perceived, no eye has seen any God besides You, who acts on behalf of those who wait for Him. But You, Lord, have revealed them unto me by Your Spirit (Isa. 64:4, NIV; 1 Cor. 2:10).

Lord, meet me as I rejoice and work righteousness (Isa. 64:5).

Lord, You are the potter, and I am the clay; I am the work of Your hand (Isa. 64:8).

I am the seed of Jacob. I am the elect, and I inherit the holy mountains and dwell there (Isa. 65:9).

I dwell in Sharon and lie down in the valley of Achor (Isa. 65:10).

I am a new creation in Christ, and my former life is not remembered, nor does it come into mind (Isa. 65:17).

I will be glad and rejoice in the new creation, for You have created Your church a rejoicing, and Your people a joy (Isa. 65:18).

Lord, You rejoice over me, and weeping and crying has departed from my life (Isa. 65:19).

I will not labor in vain, but I will enjoy the fruit of my labor, for I am the blessed of the Lord (Isa. 65:21–23).

Before I call, You will answer; and while I am yet speaking, You will hear (Isa. 65:24).

You have caused the Jew and Gentile [wolf and lamb] to feed together in Your church, and the dust is the serpent's meat. There is no hurt or destruction in Your holy mountain (Isa. 65:25).

Rejoice in Jerusalem [the church], and be glad with her, all you who love her. Rejoice for joy with her, all you who mourn for her (Isa. 66:10).

Lord, extend peace [*shalom*] to Your church like a river (Isa. 66:12).

My heart rejoices and my bones flourish like an herb, and the hand of the Lord is made known to me (Isa. 66:14).

I come to the mountain of the Lord, to Zion, and I offer myself as a living sacrifice (Isa. 66:20).

I am a priest and a Levite because of the new covenant, and the new creation, and I am a worshiper (Isa. 66:21–23).

Lord, I trust in You. Let me be as a tree planted by the waters that spreads my roots by the river, so I need not fear when heat comes. Let my leaf be green, and keep me worry-free in the year of drought, never failing to bear fruit (Jer. 17:7–8, NIV).

Lord, You are the branch of David; reign and prosper, and execute judgment and justice in the earth (Jer. 23:5).

You are the Lord our righteousness; I am saved, and I dwell safely (Jer. 23:6).

You have redeemed me and ransomed me from those who are stronger than me (Jer. 31:11).

Let me come and sing on the heights of Zion, and rejoice in the goodness of the Lord who supplies me with wheat, wine, and oil. My soil will be like a well-watered garden, and I will not sorrow anymore at all (Jer. 31:12).

Lord, satisfy my soul with abundance, and fill me with Your goodness (Jer. 31:14).

Lord, through the new covenant, put Your law in my mind, and write it upon my heart (Jer. 31:33, NIV).

Lord, search out Your sheep and take care of them. Rescue them and bring them back from the foreign nations where they now live. Be their shepherd and let them graze on fertile fields and be safe on grassy meadows and green hills. Bring back the ones that wander off; bandage those that are hurt and protect the ones that are weak (Ezek. 34:11–16, CEV).

Let Your showers of blessing be released upon my life in this season (Ezek. 34:26).

Lord, sprinkle the nations, and give the people a new heart and a new spirit; put Your spirit in them, and let them keep Your statutes and judgments (Ezek. 36:25–27).

Let Your covenant of peace continue from generation to generation, and let Your sanctuary be established in our midst (Ezek. 37:26–27).

Lord, magnify Yourself and sanctify Yourself, and let the nations know that You are the Lord (Ezek. 38:23).

Let the river of life flow from Your dwelling place throughout the nations, and let the nations be healed (Ezek. 47).

Let the nations eat from the trees of life, and let them be for medicine (Ezek. 47:12).

Lord, I am a saint, and I possess the kingdom (Dan. 7:22).

Let the sovereignty, power, and greatness of the kingdoms under the whole heaven be handed over to the saints, the people of the Most High (Dan. 7:27, NIV).

Lord, You came to make an end of sins and to establish Your kingdom (Dan. 9:24).

Lord, You came to bring in everlasting righteousness and establish Your kingdom (Dan. 9:24).

Lord, You came to seal up the vision and prophecy and to establish Your kingdom (Dan. 9:24).

Lord, You came to anoint the Most Holy and to establish Your kingdom (Dan. 9:24).

Lord, I have obtained mercy; I belong to You, and You are my God (Hosea 2:23).

Let whoever calls upon You be saved; let them come to mount Zion and be delivered (Joel 2:32).

Let the people know that You are the Lord God dwelling in Zion, the holy mountain (Joel 3:17).

Let no strangers pass through Zion anymore (Joel 3:17).

Let the mountains drip with new wine into my life (Joel 3:18).

Let the hills flow with milk into my life (Joel 3:18).

Let the rivers of Judah [praise] flood my life (Joel 3:18).

Let Your fountain come forth from the church and water the valley of Shittim (Joel 3:18, KJV).

Let Judah [praise] dwell in my life forever, and Your church from generation to generation (Joel 3:20).

Lord, You have raised up the tabernacle of David and repaired its damages, and raised up its ruins, as in the days of old; let the nations come into it (Amos 9:11; Acts 15:14–17).

Let Your church possess the remnant of Edom, and all the nations, which are called by Your name (Amos 9:12).

Let my life yield such a harvest that I won't be able to bring in all of my wheat before plowing time, and that I have grapes left over from season to season, a fruitful vineyard that covers the mountains (Amos 9:13, CEV).

Let us rebuild our towns and live in them. May we drink wine from our own vineyards and eat the fruit we grow (Amos 9:14, CEV).

Plant my roots deep in the land You have given me, so that I will never be uprooted again (Amos 9:15, CEV).

Let the nations receive deliverance on Mount Zion, and let them walk in holiness; let us possess our possessions (Obad. 17).

Raise up deliverers on Mount Zion, and let the Mount of Esau [the flesh] be judged, for the kingdom is the Lord's (Obad. 21).

Lord, assemble the lame, and the outcast, and the afflicted (Mic. 4:6).

Lord, You reign over us in Mount Zion, from henceforth and forever, even forever (Mic. 4:7, KJV).

Your kingdom has come to us, even the first dominion (Mic. 4:8, KJV).

Lord, You have had compassion on me and have subdued my iniquities and have cast my sins into the depths of the sea (Mic. 7:19, KJV).

Let the feet of them who preach the gospel bring good tidings and publish peace to the nations (Nah. 1:15, KJV).

Lord, You rejoice over me with gladness and singing, and You quiet me with Your love (Zeph. 3:17).

Lord, You will deal with all who afflict me, and will save the lame, and will gather those who were driven out, returning me home, and giving me praise and honor in the place of my captivity (Zeph. 3:19–20).

Let nations be joined unto You, Lord, and let them be Your people, with You dwelling in their midst (Zech. 2:11).

Lord, You are the Branch; build the temple [Your church], and rule from Your throne (Zech. 6:12–13).

Lord, You dwell in the midst of Your church, the city of truth, the mountain of the LORD of hosts (Zech. 8:3).

Lord, dwell in my life in truth and righteousness (Zech. 8:8).

Lord, speak peace to the nations, and let Your dominion be from sea to sea, and from the river to the ends of the earth (Zech. 9:10).

Lord, let us be as jewels in a crown, lifted up as a banner over the land (Zech. 9:16).

Lord, how great is Your goodness, and how great is Your beauty (Zech. 9:17).

Let Your fountain flow to the nations for sin and uncleanness (Zech. 13:1).

Let Your living waters flow from the church, and be our King over all the earth (Zech. 14:8–9).

Lord, let the nations come and worship You and keep the Feast of Tabernacles (Zech. 14:16).

Let the people You have gathered [tabernacles, ingathering] enjoy this time of harvest, joy, and praise (Zech. 14:16).

Let HOLINESS TO THE LORD be upon my life, and I will serve in Your house (Zech. 14:20).

Let every vessel in Your house be holy, and let us offer the sacrifices of praise (Zech. 14:21; Heb. 13:16).

Lord, You are the Sun of Righteousness; arise with healing in Your wings (Mal. 4:2).

For Yours is the kingdom and the power and the glory forever. Amen (Matt. 6:13).

Let the mysteries of the kingdom be revealed to me (Matt. 13:11).

Let men hear the word of Your kingdom and bring forth fruit (Matt. 13:23).

Let us be scribes who are instructed concerning Your kingdom (Matt. 13:52).

Lord, let Your mercy be upon those who fear You from generation to generation (Luke 1:50).

Lord, show strength with Your arm, and scatter the proud in their imagination (Luke 1:51).

Lord, put down the mighty from their thrones, and exalt the lowly (Luke 1:52).

Lord, fill the hungry with good things, and send the rich away empty (Luke 1:53).

Lord, let me be delivered out of the hand of my enemies, and let me serve You without fear, in holiness and righteousness, all the days of my life (Luke 1:74–75).

Give us power and authority over all demons, and to cure diseases, to preach the kingdom of God, and to heal the sick (Luke 9:1–2).

Lord, Your kingdom does not come with observation [not physical], but it is within us (Luke 17:20–21).

Let rivers of living water flow from my innermost being (John 7:38).

Let the word of God spread and the number of disciples be multiplied greatly (Acts 6:7).

Let signs and wonders increase in the name of Jesus (Acts 14:3).

I am a Jew, for I have been circumcised in the heart, and in the spirit, and my praise is not of men, but of God (Rom. 2:28–29).

For of Him and through Him and to Him are all things, to whom be glory forever. Amen (Rom. 11:36).

Lord, Your kingdom is not meat and drink, but righteousness, peace, and joy in the Holy Ghost (Rom. 14:17). Let Your righteousness, peace, and joy be revealed to the nations.

To God only wise, be glory through Jesus Christ for ever (Rom. 16:27).

Let Your word be preached, not with persuasive words of human wisdom, but in demonstration of the Spirit and power (1 Cor. 2:4).

Give me the spirit of wisdom and revelation in Your knowledge, and let the eyes of my understanding be enlightened to know the hope of Your calling and the riches of the glory of Your inheritance (Eph. 1:17–18).

Unto You, O God, be glory in the church through Christ Jesus throughout all ages, world without end. Amen (Eph. 3:21, KJV).

I have come to Mount Zion, to the city of the living God, the heavenly Jerusalem (Heb. 12:22).

To God our Savior, who alone is wise, be glory and majesty, dominion and power, both now and forever. Amen (Jude 25).

Let the nations [people] that are saved walk in the light of the New Jerusalem, and let the kings bring their honor and glory unto You (Rev. 21:24).